Geoff and Margaret
@RetirementTales

Retired teachers. Back on supply!

Proud to have responded to The Call!

Purveyors of Hope.

Everything you imagine us to be.

An allegory.

Rutland   Joined Twitter December 2021

Tales about schools and teaching.
A book about life and learning.

A story about hope.

Foreword

I'm assuming that you're reading this book because you're a fan of the Twitter/X account @RetirementTales. If you're not yet a fan, you soon will be...

@RetirementTales belongs to septuagenarians Geoff and Margaret. During COVID times, they answered 'The Call' from the then Education Secretary. This was for retired teachers to return to the classroom to cover staff absences. Let's not dwell on which education secretary or how many we've had since then. We'll be here all day!

Geoff and Margaret's tales of supply cover, memories of the Banda machine, online assemblies and virtual pub lunches began in December 2021. But they definitely weren't just for Christmas; they were (and continue to be) a joy to their 37k+ followers, all year round.

Teaching is a fantastic, rewarding profession. It can also be tough. Research shows that having heroes has a positive psychological impact on us, which is good for our mood, our mental health and wellbeing.

So, how did these two retirees become national teaching treasures during the pandemic? Quite simply, they became a force for positivity, offering others a place to celebrate education at the trickiest of times.

Positivity

From the get-go, no job that 'the lady from the agency' gave Geoff was too big. For example:

"Can you take a mixed-age class, primary and secondary, in a town where all the schools have no staff?"

"My pleasure!" I say.
"You will also need to cook 267 dinners..."

While it started off as a funny tweet, the reality was that people were needed to cover unexpectedly, at short notice, and teach a year group or a subject that was well out of their comfort zone. This was all while trying to keep their distance and being mindful of their 'bubbles'!

Geoff's 'keep calm and carry on' attitude helped folks to maintain perspective and not catastrophise. In schools all over the land, there was the rousing cry, 'If Geoff can do it...'

Connection

As we all know, social media can be great. It can also be foul, and #Edutwitter is a dark place sometimes. Regularly, people have said that they are having to leave, take a break or block others, for the sake of their wellbeing. While these are good decisions to make, it's a shame for the profession that not everyone can 'play nicely'.

Of course, it's okay to have a difference of opinion. However, there are ways and means (in both the real and online world) of kindly disagreeing. Geoff and Margaret reminded people how to connect in a supportive way and to: 'Keep it light and loving, and in the spirit of @RetirementTales.'

Authenticity

We all have our own image of Geoff and Margaret. In their biography on Twitter, they say that the account is an allegory and that they are, 'Everything you imagine us to be.'

I love that there has been an element of mystery about them, as I think there is about all teachers - from the minute the youngest children realise that nope, their teacher doesn't live in school and sleep in the home corner.

Whoever they really are and wherever they really live, Geoff and Margaret have a wealth of knowledge about the wonderful world of education from way-back-when. Their observational, old-school tweets have regularly made me smile, laugh and, at times, guffaw as they've taken me on their trip down memory lane.

And last, but not least...

We all love an Assembly Banger, don't we? Here's one that has had the lyrics ever so slightly tweaked:

"When we needed two heroes were you there, were you there?
When we needed two heroes were you there?
And your age and your stage (of life)
And you living in Rutland won't matter,
Were you there?"

If there was ever a song that was written for Geoff and Margaret, this is it. Although Margaret will be tutting at my disregard for the original rhythm, she'll get over it. Because these two can cope with anything and, during 2022, they helped many others cope too:

- 'Absolute sunshine on these dark mornings!'
- 'Thank you for great memories ... and a smile each day.'
- 'You've made our week!!! Thank you not only for your humour but for your friendship, understanding and camaraderie.'
- 'Thank you, thank you for making me belly laugh! You're just the tonic I need.'

Thank you, G&M!

Sarah Creegan, Former Headteacher
Founder of @lbmconsultancy
Lead Facilitator and Consultant with @laughology

Main Introduction

It was late in the autumn term, 2021.

The world was well into the second year of the
Covid-19 pandemic and schools were continuing to face
enormous disruption.

The Government launched a campaign to recruit
retired teachers back into the profession,
in an hour of great need.

In truth, not many people answered The Call.

But Geoff and Margaret did.

This is their story.

PART ONE:
THE SPRING TERM

"*Education is not preparation for life; education is life itself*".

John Dewey

PART ONE:
THE SPRING TERM

Chapter 1: The Call

The phone rings.
It's the lovely lady from the agency.
"Your first job!" she exclaims.

"Wonderful!" I reply.
"Can you take a mixed age class, primary and secondary, in a town where all the schools have no staff?"
"My pleasure!" I say.
"You will also need to cook 267 school dinners..."

♡   ⟲   ♡   ⬆

"Remind me of your specialism," the agency lady enquires.
"Geography!" I reply, eagerly.
"Fancy a day teaching music?" she asks.
"Sure! If duty calls!
Do you think they'll have a guitar for me?"
(I can do Streets of London for primary
or Big Yellow Taxi for secondary.)

♡   ⟲   ♡   ⬆

Margaret is nervous about teaching phonics again. She used Letterland for many years. She reminisces that the children loved the thrilling tales of Annie Apple and Kicking King. But poor Margaret was badly let down by Firefighter Fred in 1996. He moved out at October half term.

♡   ⟲   ♡   ⬆

An early call – on a bank holiday too!

"How about a week in Alternative Provision?" the agency lady asked. I don't honestly know what she means but it sounds like just what I need.

"Some of the pupils are runners" she says.
"Perfect!" I say. "Cross-country was one of my things!"

○   ⇄   ♡   ⬆

I am looking forward to tomorrow so very much!
I've polished my Hush Puppies, packed my lunch and double checked the shuttle bus timetable.

I've been told that, depending on who else makes it in, I'll be teaching all of Year Four or manning the school office.

Or both.

○   ⇄   ♡   ⬆

Another call from the agency! "You work on Sundays?" I ask.

Margaret has been offered all next week in Year 2, which I think she'll love!

I have the option of a Reception class til half term, two weeks in a special school or an assistant headship.

I wish I could do them all!

○   ⇄   ♡   ⬆

I feel so wanted! I've just been asked to cover three roles in one day: crossing patrol, site manager and junior teacher (mixed Years 3, 4, 5 and 6). I think I'll combine them and do some road safety teaching.

Tufty says "Never forget your kerb drill!"

Some of our lovely followers have been in touch to ask how you can book me and Margaret to work in your schools. Thank you for your interest! The best way is to contact our employment agency, Rutland Mortar:

Rutland Mortar
Employment Agency
We fill the gaps so you don't have to!

From Cottesmore to Uppingham and perhaps beyond!

"We fill the gaps so you don't have to!"

The first day of term and the first day of teaching in quite a while for me and Margaret.
Who knows what's ahead?
Such anticipation!
Margaret and I answered The Call because we wanted to make a difference.

Margaret's first day!
The school wanted to print a visitor label for her but the machine in the entrance had 17 attempts at taking her photo! She's only 4'10". In the end, they used a picture of a similar looking lady from the parish magazine and just buzzed Margaret in.

When I arrived this morning, the head greeted me so warmly again. "Geoff! You've really come back!"

"I said I would, Sir. My word is my oak!" I noticed that the head was still quite red in the face and he seemed a little out of breath. "He probably ran to school" I thought.

"Do you have a DBS, Geoff? I should have asked yesterday!" I think for a minute but I'm not sure what he means.
"I have an old TSB account but it's been dormant a while!" I respond. "That will do fine!" he replies. "Just give the long number to the ladies in the office."

Margaret called me after Pointless.
"About time!" I say.
"Yes, it is actually!" she replies.
"Geoff, I stayed for the whole day.
The children couldn't get enough of
the blank clock faces!" she exclaims.
"Or the sharp pencils!"
"Margaret, I'm proud of you!" I say.

One lesson actually turned into a full day!
There was a starter: pencil sharpening.
There was a plenary: cleaning up pencil shavings.
There was differentiation: some pupils did more than others.
It might be 2022 but Margaret still knows teaching & she still
knows children.

Today I was an artist, an architect and an engineer!
I was an inventor, a storyteller, a shepherd and a nurse.
Today I sang and imagined and laughed out loud!
Today I was surrounded by curiosity and fun. And life.

Today I taught Reception!

I'm having an early start today so that I can fit more day in!
It's been playing on my mind that we've had many calls for help.
I've told the lovely primary head I am needed elsewhere today
and I've answered The Call to a Special School.
I'm about to get on my way.

Well what a privilege today has been!
I have been immersed in love and life and learning.
And kindness and courage.
I've met the most astonishing people.
A Special School indeed!

Three weeks into extra time and I've finally returned to my geography roots! I took back to back Year 8 classes this morning. The open windows, broken heaters, high ceilings and frosty teenage glances all created a chilly climate that really suited our topic of glaciation!

Yesterday, I promised the Lovely Head I would go back and actually do some teaching today.

He's juggling many absences:
"You could literally teach anywhere, Geoff!"
"Thank you!" I replied.

I chose Year 6 and the children said they couldn't remember ever doing a WHOLE DAY of geography before!

Despite being small herself, Margaret was surprised by just how small the children were & even more surprised by the furniture! The nursery children climbed, put on over-sized clothes and ate fruit as big as their own faces.

"It was like being on the set of The Borrowers, Geoff!"

It's a wondrous thing – a gift – to learn new things at this ripe old age!
I've spent two days working in alternative provision and it's been a revelation. I've penned another little poem, this time written from a pupil's perspective.

Glad I Came Here
I came here by taxi
I came here confused
I came here "in crisis"
I came here cause I had to
I came cause it wasn't going well
I came here for a chance
I came here hurting
And they met me with Love.

French through music – c'est magnifique!
Year 7 loved Joe le Taxi! Très bon!
Year 10 REALLY enjoyed the Lady Marmalade video on YouTube.
They were transfixed!
I was struggling with Year 13 but the students later said that "Je t'aime moi non plus" was "just our kind of French!"

Chapter 3 : Banda on the Run

Bless Margaret!
This morning, she poured a miniature bottle of fluid into the "huge modern looking Banda machine."
It was her own bottle: a Banda vintage '82.
There's now a trail of purple ink from the photocopier to the staff toilet.
Margaret's best C&A tights are ruined.

"But Geoff, what is a Banda?" our younger followers have been asking.
This is a Banda!
It was how we copied worksheets and letters in another millennium.
It was manual. You needed a carbon master copy and some spirits that caused much excitement.

Margaret was in Year 2 today and she decided to teach an RE lesson on Epiphany. Like all the best RE, Margaret told the story from the Bible, then asked the children to tell her the same story back. There sadly wasn't a sheet to colour, due to the earlier Banda mishap.

One of Margaret's favourite lessons was asking children to draw the hands on clock faces! She would prepare the worksheet at home, using her clock stamper & ink pad. Margaret has prepared a new sheet for today and will ask the office to run a set through the big Banda for Year 2.

🗨   ↻   ♡   🢁

This spring, Margaret is all set to deliver a whole unit of Christianity in R.E. Using just four Ladybird books, she can teach ten different stories about Jesus. "One a week from January to Easter!" {Margaret always reserves the last two weeks for palm branches & Easter bonnets.)

🗨   ↻   ♡   🢁

Margaret has already decided on an activity for this week.
It suits all ages!
It's a favourite in any class!
It's fine motor control.
It's hand/eye co-ordination.
It's technology & science.
It's history.
It's her old hand-winding pencil sharpener!
"They'll be queueing up, Geoff!"

         🢁

TOPIC TIME:

THE BANDA MACHINE

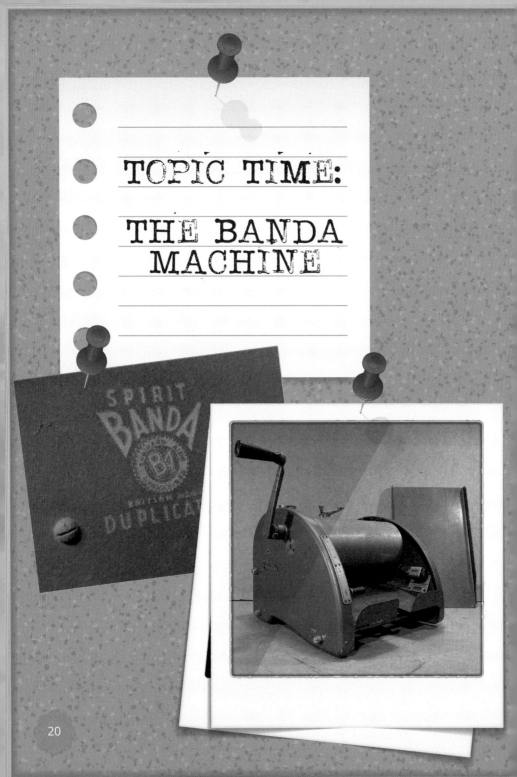

Topic Time: The Banda Machine

Unless you're of a certain vintage, like me and Margaret, you might not be familiar with the term "Banda machine". However, the trusted Banda machine was a stalwart of school life for decades. It was there in the background, a work-horse, producing the resources which were used in class every day, in a world before photocopiers, computers and Google. You might not have remembered the name but the chances are you do remember what the Banda machine gave you: those A4 sheets of purple clock faces; the school newsletters and Nativity play scripts written on a typewriter and copied in strong smelling ink. If you remember your teacher handing out a worksheet and instantly holding it up to your nose, then you do know what a Banda is!

The Banda was a type of spirit duplicator – a manual photocopier, if you will. The word 'spirit' is a little clue as to why this particular artefact stirs such vivid memories, for alcohol was a significant ingredient in the inks which were used in these machines. The Banda machine used a printing method which had been invented in the early 1920s and which became popular due to the relative ease and low cost of copying. There were other manufacturers of spirit duplicators around the world (including Rexograph, Ditto and Gestetner) but it was the name "Banda" which became synonymous with worksheets and handouts in schools around Great Britain. It also became synonymous with the colour purple, or aniline purple, to be precise.

These days, you can run off multiple copies of a resource or document by pressing just a few buttons on a photocopier. The Banda machine required a little more time and patience. The teacher would prepare a resource for their class. It might be a picture to colour, a diagram to label, a map, a spelling test or even an exam paper. This original copy would then be attached to a second sheet which was coated in a layer of wax. The two-ply spirit master copy would then be sent through the Banda, making a printing plate on the drum of the machine. The teacher could then run off a class set, in the colour or colours of their choice. A good quality master copy could usually produce up to about 40 decent copies, enough for even the largest of classes in days gone by.

School pupils have always enjoyed the honour of being a monitor. In Banda times, being a class monitor meant you had the luxury of distributing worksheets to your classmates whilst also smelling the freshly printed Banda fluid. What a treat! Children pretended to get high from the potent smell. Teachers reminded pupils that "getting high" was not to be joked about.

But, in truth, everybody loved that smell!

Memories of the Banda Machine

Oh how we loved the smell of the Banda machine.
And the lovely purple colour. The smell and the colour sort of
grew together and became the same thing in my mind. That's
what solvents can do to a seven year old.
@elizabennet3

As a student teacher the joy of having five different
coloured carbon sheets and working until 2am to create
one multi-coloured worksheet –
#theworldbeforecomputers
@KarenHudspith

When I was at primary school, turning the handle of the Banda
was a reward. You got to walk down to "the new unit" and stand
turning the handle while envious others walked past.
@leftylloyd

It was surprising how long a master copy could last if you were
careful. I was called the Banda Queen at one school. The only
animals I could draw with any reliability were hedgehogs so
they always appeared somewhere, however irrelevant.
@Harper1Suzanne

You could spot teachers in the supermarket by their purple hands.
@seainclusion

Oh, the memories, the aroma, the fun we had...
A much simpler existence.
Now, I am known as the photocopier whisperer.
I have a knack of sorting out the machine when
It has a hissy fit. I always talk to it nicely and give
it a "thank you" pat on the lid when it's done a
good job.
@Gileragirl

I met my future husband when he showed
me how to work the Banda machine in 1983.
@gerrywhite2

I remember helping to print my
school's newsletters on the Banda
when I was in Year 6.

It was the highest honour!
@kezwick_98765

Chapter 4: #BeMoreMargaret

Margaret has just been offered two weeks of teaching in a nursery class. The agency lady asked if she knew about "in the moment planning".

This shouldn't be a problem.

Margaret taught for 38 years and she never spent more than a moment planning anything.

♡   ⟲   ♡   ↑

I check my phone.
12 missed calls, 7 voicemails and 4 texts.
All Margaret.
She's had a change of heart!
Across the messages, she mentions
tights and visitor photos and the Banda.
But best of all: "It's for the children.
I think they need me."

6th January is Margaret's Epiphany.

♡   ⟲   ♡   ↑

It might be the weekend but Margaret has been thinking about school while she's been watching repeats of Heartbeat.

Margaret has just phoned to tell me about her idea!

Her friend, Sandra, has a son who is a police dog handler.
"He's a Bobby, Geoff.
And a bobby-dazzler!"

Margaret taught a popular "Emergency" topic every year. A policeman would visit and pretend to be "a baddie" – chased across the field by his German Shepherd.

Margaret wants Sandra's son to make
this happen again in 2022.

As well as Pointless, Margaret loves The Chase.

Margaret has been reluctant to tell me how her morning went. It turns out, she wasn't prepared for a fire drill.

She says she was very pleased to get everyone out safely and she did account for the right number of children. It's just that they weren't all from the right class.

Margaret was back in Year 1 today. As she'd learned the ropes yesterday, she managed time well; the twelve minute phonics lesson was "more than enough!"
She followed this with a traffic survey in maths and, by lunch, the children were proficient with digraphs, trigraphs and bar graphs!

💬　⟲　♡　⬆

Well it sounds like Margaret the infant teacher is quite the Year 3 convert!

"The children got in & out of their own coats!
Nobody asked "is this literacy or numeracy?"

Best of all:

"Some children were so capable that they wrote the long date and still had time to do their work!"

💬　⟲　♡　⬆

Earlier in the week, one of our followers asked our opinion on classroom displays.

Margaret recalls a time in her school when everything on display had to be double or triple mounted.

Margaret did as much mounting as possible at home. It helped her to keep on top of things.

💬　⟲　♡　⬆

Margaret is in good spirits!
Hairdresser Natalie told Margaret that her new look was "on point". She will be living off that compliment for a few weeks!

Margaret has a new hair style, a new cardigan, many new friends and a new love of teaching.

No longer a sundial in the shade...!

💬   🔁   ♡   ⬆

Margaret has been offered two days of work in Year 1.

She's very excited about being in school again for Shrove Tuesday!

No, she hasn't done a risk assessment.
No, she isn't a first aider.
No, she doesn't know if the oven has been PAT tested.
But yes, she will be making pancakes.

💬   🔁   ♡

The Staff Room

In the old days, there was time each day for a nice cup of tea and a sit down.

At morning break, teachers would enjoy a KitKat or maybe even a cigarette.

Margaret left me a voicemail message earlier. She'd just come out of adult craft club but she can't stop thinking about teaching children!

"Geoff! It's me! Are you there...?
I've got craft ideas for Mothering Sunday and Easter!

...Do you think they sell Binca on Amazon, Geoff?"

Remember when there was a stencil for everything?

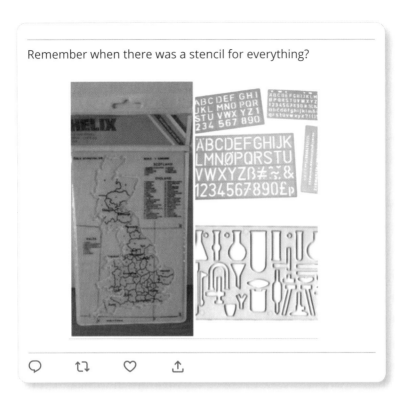

Margaret has been in the mixed Year 1/2 class again.

She would have happily left the computer off but "apparently, there's no other way of doing the register!"

Margaret thinks this is ridiculous.

She knows another way of doing the register.

Margaret was a big fan
of the rolling blackboard!

Being rather short, she
liked the fact that she
could write on the board
without needing a step.

"SMART boards are
all very well but they
don't cater for different
heights, Geoff!"

Tobacco in a school?
Es in a tin?
The drugs don't work.
Just say no!
(Or "nope" if you're
learning about
the magic "e".)

Margaret has been reminiscing about the late 90s, when a new by-law meant that teachers had to have WordArt on signs all over their classrooms.

Margaret was given a sign for her door which said: "Literacy Hour in Progress – Do Not Disturb!"

Margaret didn't like the late 90s.

Margaret wonders if anybody else remembers Richard Scarry's books?

This one was in her classroom reading corner – enjoyed by a great many children, over the years!

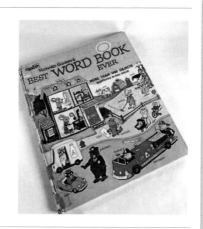

Margaret says she's had a splendid day:
"We've been immersed in rhyme and story-telling, Geoff!"

In the morning, Margaret shared two special books: When We
Were Very Young by A.A. Milne (from her childhood) and
The Jolly Postman by Janet & Allan Ahlberg (from her career).
-
In the afternoon, Margaret knew only one book would do. She
read Dogger by Shirley Hughes.

"We laughed and we worried, and we cried and we celebrated
together, Geoff. It was magical!"

◯   ⇅   ♡   ↥

I told Margaret that some of our followers have been asking
our thoughts on staff well-being.

"There has always been 'well-being', Geoff!
It's just that it used to go by other names."

Two synonyms spring straight to Margaret's mind:

"The firefighters' visit" and "Friday pub lunch".

◯   ⇅   ♡   ↥

Topic Time: The Friday Pub Lunch

Let me take you back in time. Let me take you back to a time when schools were very different and, specifically, when the lunch period was very different.

It was a time when lunch was actually long enough to be a break for everyone. It was a time when some children went home for their midday meal and when most teachers headed to the staffroom.

It was a time when it was ok to pause and rest, to enjoy time with family, classmates or colleagues. It was a time when, as a teacher, you could actually enjoy a warm brew, eat your lunch and still have time for marking, running clubs or doing jobs in the classroom.

Topic Time: The Friday Pub Lunch

It was in that time that there existed one of the greatest well-being initiatives the profession has ever seen: the Friday Pub Lunch! It's almost impossible to conceive now but, for a great many teachers, over a great many years, a highlight of the working week was a staff trip to the pub on a Friday. A quick drink or two? Sure! A tasty bar meal? Why not?! Some jukebox tunes and a game of pool or darts? Yes please!

This is how it worked. Schools would usually have a regular pub or pubs which their staff would head to. Timing was key, so preparation was important. It was always best to phone through the food orders in advance. This meant you got served quickly on arrival. People knew the menus well and they tended to stick with the classics: a jacket potato, a baguette or chicken in a basket. You needed to get to the pub quickly so it was preferable to arrange the transport meticulously. You needed to know who was driving and whose car you were going in. You headed to the car park as quickly as possible at the sound of the bell and you avoided any distractions on the way through the school corridors. If somebody's car was blocked in, there might have to be a last-minute change of designated drivers. There was no time to waste!

When you arrived at the pub on a Friday lunchtime, there was a celebratory feeling – you had almost made it through another week at school! Sure, you still had to teach double German, deliver an infant art lesson or sit through an end-of-week assembly but first there would be drink, food, music, laughter and, most importantly of all, camaraderie.

With it being one of the highlights of the week, it was important to get as much as possible out of the pub lunch experience. This meant leaving just the right amount of time for the journey back to school. Of course, everybody knew how many minutes the drive would take and what time they needed to set off by. But things didn't always go to plan. Sometimes, teachers would arrive back at school a little late for the afternoon session. In that instance, they avoided the main entrance, if they could. They might have had to apologise to an unimpressed dinner lady or thank the student who took the register for them.

Memories of the Friday Pub Lunch

I remember those days. All quite normal and respectable. My first year teaching was Friday pub lunch followed by swimming at the local pool.
Best working day ever!
@thorpe-anna

Absolutely was a well-being thing before well-being was a thing. So many happy memories of my first years of teaching in the early 90s. Many spontaneous Friday lunches out. Teaching is very different now.
@pollybassi

Ahh, I remember it well! We'd phone ahead to order food so we had time to eat it before getting back to school! All was well till a 6 yr old in my class told me my breath smelt like his dad's when he came back from the pub! I had orange juice after that.
@k8r3n

I had some great laughs on Friday lunchtime at the pub when I was a teacher. I had music club lunches, running club lunches, tuition lunches, but Friday was the pub!
@JonSmit96578842

Thanks for reminding us. We went to the Deans house in Prescot, up the road from Huyton, Liverpool. Wonderful children. That Friday hour was the real staff meeting. All we talked was school and planning the next school trip. Loved the job! @rosaleenmward

I miss the pub lunches too! Such fond memories! Half of Broadside whilst I waited for my bar meal, served outside under the gazebo, staying as long as possible, then running back and up four flights of stairs for afternoon registration. @year5rocks

Friday pub lunch was amazing! We had a choice of three pubs we could walk to in five mins! Headteacher at my last school locked four of us out of school for going to the butty shop without permission!
(We'd been going to the butty shop for 13 years.)
@loulou0706

In my first school we all went to the "library" on Friday lunch times. Children often asked where my books were....
I always said I'd left them in my car.
@spelky67

Chapter 6: A Little aPolitical

Margaret finished off the week by telling her class the fable of The Boy Who Cried Wolf.

To bring the story up to date, she renamed the boy Prince Novak of Johnsonland.

Margaret can do traditional and contemporary at the same time.

💬 🔁 ♡ ↥

Margaret told two Bible stories today:
Feeding the Five Thousand & Water into Wine.

"Margaret, you taught about large gatherings with food & drink?" I asked, nervously.

"It wasn't political, Geoff!" she replied.
"They're religious allegories.

This was Galilee, not Downing Street!"

💬 🔁 ♡ ↥

Margaret taught The Last Supper in RE today.
I don't know if she's using her Ladybird books or a local syllabus. Either way, she's very early for Easter!
"It was the meeting of all meetings, Geoff.
There was food, drink and a sense of finality."

Margaret is quite the theologian!

💬 🔁 ♡ ↥

Margaret says that the Education Secretary doesn't have enough sensible ideas to write a haiku, never mind a White Paper.

I've reminded Margaret that we are supposed to be apolitical.

"Plain white paper would be more beneficial to the profession right now, Geoff!" she added.

01 Apr 22

Margaret has taken it upon herself to write a haiku in response to the White Paper.

It's called "A Little aPolitical"

Even in April
Education must not be
Led by Mindless Fools

Here's a classic story about a group of boys stranded on an island and their disastrous attempts to govern themselves.

There's tension between individuality and group thinking, rational and emotional reactions, and between morality & immorality.

Margaret says it sounds familiar...

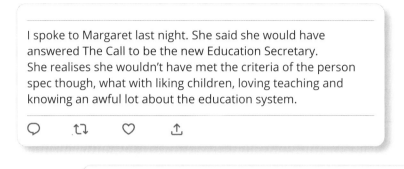

I spoke to Margaret last night. She said she would have answered The Call to be the new Education Secretary.
She realises she wouldn't have met the criteria of the person spec though, what with liking children, loving teaching and knowing an awful lot about the education system.

Margaret and I have very much enjoyed returning to the classroom but we're truly concerned by the immense pressure on children, staff and schools in 2022. We've taken the liberty of writing a manifesto for education. It's a GEM from G & M.

Geoff and Margaret's Great Education Manifesto 2022

Although Margaret and I are rather fond of looking back, we are not averse to looking forward! Sure, we're relics from another era but we want you and your children to be the pioneers. Education is the profession that creates all others; it's our shared duty to shape the future!

So, here's a manifesto for education in 2022! It's the simple thoughts of two septuagenarians who have spent a lifetime in primary and secondary, and a term of retirement in pandemic-hit schools:

1. Invest in children and students of all ages!
2. Invest in, and care for, all those who work in childcare and education!
3. Remove unnecessary forces at this time of extraordinary disruption!

These three proposals are connected by a central theme: Well-being. We must prioritise well-being now, in order to preserve education for the future.

NB: We did have three main proposals but then Margaret thought of "just one more thing". She's been watching a lot of Columbo, of late.

4. Reform the Department for Education.
Better still, remove education from politics!

Chapter 7: "It's Got Pockets, Geoff!"

Margaret has decided she won't wear her waterfall cardigan if she's in Nursery again. There's salt dough in the cable knit and the smart belt buckle is strangely sticky.

She's still in good spirits though.
She's been listening to Cliff Richard on shuffle and now she's wired for sound.

💬　🔁　♡　↥

Margaret has just called. She's had an Amazon delivery! At the recommendation of some of our followers, she's treated herself to a heated gilet.

Margaret says she's thrilled with the fit and style but she's not sure how she'll get it PAT tested in time for school on Monday.

💬　🔁　♡　↥

During the half term break, Margaret enjoyed a bit of internet shopping. She'd had a few recommendations from our followers and had something very specific in mind for her work wardrobe.

Margaret's new Popsy dress has arrived today. She sounds elated:
"It's got pockets, Geoff!"

💬　🔁　♡　↥

Margaret is wearing her new dress with pockets today. She says it's taken far too long to recognise that women's clothing can be smart and practical too. She says not having pockets is a symbol of male patriarchy. #InternationalWomensDay

Margaret is putting her feet up after a non-stop day in Nursery. She's "a bit perplexed" by what she's found in the pockets of her Popsy dress:
The pen from the interactive board;
a couple of marbles;
a mitten;
a Pritt Stick lid;
a triangular Stickle Brick &
a tissue (not hers).

Margaret was in a school today where they had "Mini Police" on duty at lunchtime. Margaret thinks she would like to be in the Mini Police herself. Well, if the cap fits. (It will fit. She's 4ft 10.)

Margaret has just called again. She could barely speak! Her friend, Sandra, has just offered her a ticket to see The Osmonds Musical in Leicester, tomorrow afternoon. Margaret's having hot flushes at the prospect of going! She should perhaps switch off her heated gilet now.

Chapter 8: Nursery Nurse Doris

When Margaret arrived in Reception today, long-serving nursery nurse, Doris, was already there.

Doris told Margaret "This is my half of the room. That's your half."

"I don't go outside and I don't do messy!" she added.

Margaret joked "There is no 'i' in team but there is in Doris".

💬   🔁   ♡   ↑

Margaret was in VERY early today.
She decided to change things a bit.
She set up both halves of the classroom entirely with messy play.
Everything else was outside.
It was a masterclass in transforming practice.
"The children were in their element, Geoff!"

Doris chose inside.

💬   🔁   ♡   ↑

Margaret has rescheduled her chiropodist appointment so she can return to Reception today. She's already set up the class and Doris will be outside.
("It's a non-negotiable, Geoff!")

💬   🔁   ♡   ↑

It was a little frosty this morning, both inside & out.
But it was Margaret who began the thawing process.

"Doris, it's not about me being right nor you being wrong.
It's about children. It's about letting learning happen."

Margaret is truly Early Years, even in her Later Years.

Margaret spent one last day in Reception, for now at least.

It was cold and wet so Margaret and Doris shared the duties inside and out. They decided to forgo the virtual pub and instead ate their lunch together in the classroom.

They reminisced about the old days in education.

If ever she's asked back, Margaret has promised to show Doris her vintage ink stamps and her classic Ladybird books.

Doris has promised Margaret she will do some messy play, occasionally.

"I'm letting learning happen" she said.

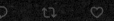

Still exhausted from making 28
Mothering Sunday cards last week,
Margaret let Doris take the lead with
Easter cards today. It was a team effort
to get the lid off the PVA glue but,
by lunchtime, it was sticky everywhere.

"Those pesky little glue spreaders!"
exclaimed Margaret.

Margaret's had a tricky day.

Nursery Nurse Doris was off ill so Margaret had no support.
"Geoff, taking a Reception class by yourself is not easy! It's
like plaiting fog when you're up the creek, without a paddle!"

Margaret doesn't mince her words but she does mix her
metaphors.

Chapter 9: The Old School Assembly

Due to popular demand, this week's Friday Virtual Pub Lunch will be followed immediately by an end of term assembly.

It will be old school hymns only.

Margaret has kindly offered to play piano, if we can get it tuned in time.

Come and Praise!

💬   🔁   ♡   ⬆️

I've been back in my regular primary school today.

The Lovely Head was delighted to see me and he was thrilled to hear of our nostalgic assembly plans!

He's offered us an overhead projector and a broken ring binder of acetates, with hymns which used to be in alphabetical order.

💬   🔁   ♡   ⬆️

Margaret has decided not to take any supply work today but she's still going into school! She's got to get some "serious" piano practice and she's really hoping Doris has got a copy of Come & Praise.

"Geoff, we've had 91 hymn suggestions.
Two are in rounds and one is in Welsh."

💬   🔁   ♡   ⬆️

Doris greeted Margaret with a proud smile.

Not only had she found a copy of Come & Praise but she'd also dusted the piano! Before sitting down, Margaret peeped in the piano stool and found a copy of the book "Merrily to Bethlehem'.

Looks like we'll all be here 'til Christmas...

💬   🔁   ♡   ↥

The Lovely Head really came up trumps today! He gave us use of the old canteen and provided some "capable" Year 5 pupils to sort the song acetates.

He personally wheeled the piano from the main hall and, at lunch, he brought the Year 3 Recorder Club, to try out one of Margaret's ideas.

💬   🔁   ♡   ↥

The Old School Assembly

Margaret and I are thrilled to reveal the song selection and running order for our assembly! We've tried to pick hymns from different eras and to include a range of styles.

Margaret has another day of practice ahead. She's the epitome of dedication!

💬   🔁   ♡   ↥

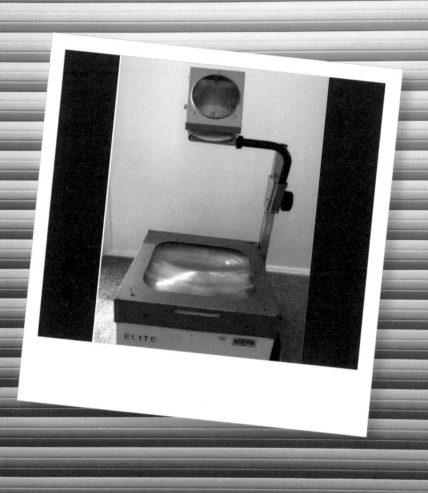

Geoff and Margaret's Old School Assembly
Friday 11th February, 2022

Entry Music: Jerusalem

1. All Things Bright and Beautiful 🌼 (Recorders)

2. When I Needed a Neighbour 🖤

3. When A Knight Won His Spurs ⚔️

4. Colours of Day (Light Up The Fire) 🔥

5. Lord of the Dance 🕺

6. He's Got The Whole World in His Hands 🌍🫴
(with actions)

7. Streets of London 🕸️ (w. Geoff on Guitar 🎸)

8. Will Your Anchor Hold In The Storms of Life? ⚓

9. From The Tiny Ant 🐜

10. Autumn Days 🍃✈️

11. Calon Lan 🔥

12. If I Were A Butterfly 🦋 (Percussion)

Closing Prayer (The Lovely Head)

Exit Music: Lord, Dismiss Us With Thy Blessing

*The end of term
and the end of part one*

PART TWO:
THE SUMMER TERM

"The beautiful thing about learning is that no-one can take it away from you"

B.B. King

PART TWO:
THE SUMMER TERM

It's the summer term!
Margaret has a few ideas of things she'd like to do, should the opportunity arise. In particular, if any schools are doing Maypole dancing and find themselves short-staffed, Margaret will gladly step in (and out) at very short notice.

You can count on her.

Margaret was really excited to find this afternoon's plans for Year 2 included a science lesson on circuit making.

"I felt like Johnny Ball, for a moment there!" she said.

Alas, the moment didn't last long. Poor Margaret ended up feeling more like Old Mother Hubbard.

Like most primary school teachers before her, Margaret went to the science cupboard only to find a sorry selection of Never Ready batteries, broken crocodile clips and enough bulbs for the children to work in groups of ten.

"They were supposed to be working in pairs, Geoff."

"How do you feel about a day of secondary school English, Geoff?" the agency lady asked.
"That would be novel" I replied.
"Or novels!" she retorted, wittily.
She was right too.

It was Animal Farm with Year 8 and Lord of the Flies with Year 9. Literally.

💬   ⟲   ♡   ⬆

Today's plans included circle time in PSHE.
Margaret likes the idea of circle time but she wonders if the person who invented it had ever taught Year 1.
It took 20 minutes to move the furniture and another 20 just to form a circle.

"It was supposed to be a half hour lesson, Geoff!"

💬   ⟲   ♡   ⬆

The school where Margaret taught at today still has a tannoy, with speakers everywhere!

Margaret found this out during maths, when there was this announcement: "Can the owner of the Nissan Leaf please move it now so the bin lorry can get in?"

"It seemed more glamorous in Rydell High, Geoff!"

💬   ⟲   ♡   ⬆

There was high drama in Margaret's school first thing!

Somebody had gone looking for border rolls but instead they found a chalk outline of a body on the stockroom floor.

A note said:
"This is what will happen to the next person who leaves the sugar paper piles in this mess!"

Schools are actually an underworld of moderate crime.

It was always thus.

From the sneaky laminator pouch thief to the rogue who leaves dirty mugs everywhere.

From the maverick who props open their fire door to the colleague who never has the cash for the staff lottery.

Chapter Two: Maths Mastery

The headteacher at Margaret's current school is "very young and very welcoming".

She kindly invited Margaret to join the staff meeting after school!

"It's all about Maths Mastery!" the head enthused.

"Have you heard of it?"

Margaret told her she's been mastering maths since 1972...

💬   🔁   ♡   ⬆️

Margaret was thrilled by today's maths work: measurement.

The teacher had emailed the plans but Margaret ignored them and headed straight for the Unifix tray.

By 9.25, there were cubes everywhere and children measuring everything, everywhere!

Margaret does non-standard very well.

💬   🔁   ♡   ⬆️

Building on the children's recent learning, there was only one thing for it today: the trundle wheel!
Margaret measured a child lying down (1 click) and the classroom (7 clicks).
Then everyone went out and lost count of the clicks on the playground.

"It's massive!" they conceded.

Margaret has been back to the maths cupboard today.
"It's like an educational emporium, Geoff…" she said, "…and a Tardis!"

Margaret only went in for some coloured pegs and boards but she came out with three trundle wheels, two sorting hoops and a tray of plastic coins.

The deputy head greeted me by asking if I would mind covering some maths this morning.
"Sure, but I'm no mathematician!" I replied. In truth, trigonometry was a stretch for some of Year 10 and for me, though calculators are a big improvement on the tables I learned with!

In the 1980s, primary school maths lessons often began with the words "Open your Hesse workbooks!" If you finished early, you could just do another page or two.

You could sometimes ask for help but the teacher also had a queue of readers to get through...

  ♡

Margaret was in Year 1 today. It was number bonds in maths but Margaret really wasn't impressed by the children's number formation.
"It wasn't pretty at all, Geoff!" she said.

Of course, Margaret knew exactly who could make things better.

Answering The Call since 1993:
El Nombre!

♡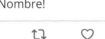

Having watched "quite a lot" of El Nombre, Margaret thought it would be good for the children themselves to write numbers in the sand. Alas, the large outdoor sandpit had a lid and a padlock.

Margaret says she can only imagine what crimes led to this level of sandpit security.

  ♡

Chapter Three: She is D.I.S.C.O.

At lunchtime today, there was a conversation about grammar in the staff room. The Literacy Leader asked Margaret if she knew what a fronted adverbial was!

Margaret was affronted herself.
"Before you were even born, I was using adverbials left, right and centre!" Margaret replied.

💬   ♺   ♡   ⬆

Margaret's had a great day in Nursery!
The TA introduced her to something called "Dough Disco".
Margaret is rather taken by it!
In fact,
She is D: doing more tomorrow
She is I: improving motor control
She is S: smelling of Play-Doh
She is C: co-ordinated
She is O: oh, oh...

💬   ♺   ♡   ⬆

Margaret's second Dough Disco was thwarted by a "cheeky chap" who wasn't happy about leaving the sand tray. Margaret did manage to coax him away eventually, though he insisted on taking most of the sand with him.

The TA has kindly offered to make a new batch of dough tonight.

💬   ♺   ♡   ⬆

Margaret was confused by a "Cultural Capital" display in the corridor today. She's visited the Cultural Quarter in Leicester and the capital city too. She's seen Culture Club in concert. She's spent a lifetime teaching about capital letters.

The display wasn't about any of these.

◯   ⇄   ♡   ⬆

Margaret's Year 1 class had "Golden Time" this afternoon, including a half hour slot in the library. The children loved it but Margaret wonders if the class teacher is off due to the stress of changing 30 children's books in 30 minutes.

"It was like Challenge Anneka, Geoff!"

◯   ⇄   ♡   ⬆

Margaret is amazed by advancements in technology. Her class today used an art app on iPads, to practise their drawing skills. It's not all gains though. By the time everyone had logged in, Margaret could easily have prepared thirty sets of tracing paper and heard six readers.

◯   ⇄   ♡   ⬆

There was an LA advisor in Margaret's school today. He'd come to carry out a "mock deep dive" in English. Margaret understands monitoring but she doesn't like the water metaphor or the pressure. She thinks the advisor should have worn sub-aqua gear rather than a sharp suit.

◯   ⇄   ♡   ⬆

TOPIC TIME:
THE MOBILE CLASSROOM

Margaret and I would like to offer
our condolences to anybody who
ever worked or studied in a
mobile classroom.
"It'll just be for one year!" the head said...

Ah, the mobile classroom! The education equivalent of a conservatory! Far too hot in the summer. Far too cold in the winter. Part of the school and yet not quite part of the school. Loved by some. Loathed by others!

The mobile classroom has a long history in our nation's schools and colleges and examples can still be found on school sites all over the country. From pre-school settings to sixth form bases, the mobile classroom has been designated as a learning environment for pupils of all ages. Sometimes it's been intended as a temporary solution. Sometimes "temporary" has turned out to be 60 years. That's "temporary" as in fifteen Olympic cycles...

Topic Time: The Mobile Classroom

Depending on where you lived or when you studied or taught in a mobile classroom, you might know this type of classroom by another name. Some called them The Terrapins, The Huts and The Sheds. Others referred to them as The Portacabins or The Demountables – names as clunky and child-friendly as the buildings themselves. For others, these "temporary" buildings were known as The Elliot Hut, the ROSLA Block or The HORSA Hut. These latter names take us back to the reason why many such structures ended up on the nation's playgrounds.

The Education Act 1944 set out that the school leaving age should increase by a year, to age 15. This compulsory requirement meant that there was an urgent need to house more than 150,000 additional pupils in secondary schools around the country. In addition to this change, there were two other significant factors affecting school capacity and premises in the second half of the 1940s. Firstly, many school buildings had been damaged or lost in World War II. Secondly, there was the matter of the post-war baby boom.

In order to support the extension of compulsory school education, the Government needed to support the extension of schools themselves. They did this by developing a programme called the "Hutting Operation for Raising of the School-Leaving Age" or HORSA, for short. The scale of the HORSA programme was unprecedented, with prefabricated "huts" adding 7000 new classrooms and being part of almost a thousand new primary schools by the end of the 1940s.

In the decades that followed, schools continued to have a need for affordable extra spaces and portacabins popped up everywhere. Sometimes, additional classrooms were needed while a school underwent refurbishment or while new facilities were built. Sometimes, they were needed to house children from a "bulge" year group or due to the expansion of a particular department. Whatever the reason, those HORSA Huts, Terrapins and all types of mobile classroom became a familiar fixture of school for generations of children and teachers.

A temporary fixture, of course...

Memories of the Mobile Classroom

In 1991-1993, I taught in a mobile classroom that had been set up in 1946 and condemned as unsafe sometime in the mid-1980s.
@seainclusion

I loved teaching in one. It was well-kitted out and so spacious! It was during a massive refurbishment and our old rooms were open plan. The head used to slide up on you like Nosferatu but he couldn't surprise us in the mobile classroom.
Having a door was the best thing!
@PigeonHips

I loved my "mobile" classroom. I had my best Year 6 in there and they made Passport Control at the door!
We made ourselves an independent state!
@kazza-cupcake

It was 25 years for me. When our dilapidated school was finally rebuilt and I got to teach a lesson "indoors", I was awarded the Ernest Shackleton award for enduring suffering!
@IantoMitch

One teacher I knew, a keen fisherman, left a dead pike under his mobile and forgot about it. Returning after half term, the stench inside was beyond belief.
@suemonkman29

We got an art teacher after the head told them we had plans for a purpose built art block. 10 years later, all spent in a temp classroom, we built the art block.
@neileley

My mum taught in an Elliot. She loved it as no-one came and "borrowed" things from her cupboard. She didn't like the long walk to the loo though and she shared an illicit kettle with the teacher in the other half.
@lucyfrearson

The whole of my teaching career took place in one of these.
Downside: no water, chilly in winter.
Upside: no-one else could hear the noise.
@revmaryhawes

I taught Year 8 "Goodnight Mister Tom" in one of these. When learning about evacuees and the consequent overcrowding in village schools, one of the children said, gesturing to the portacabin around us,
"You'd think things would've improved by now..."
@Camelgod3

The mobile classroom was there when I was a pupil (1977-1981) and still there when I returned as a teacher in 2005...
@juliedearness

For a year I taught some classes in a "Terrapin". It had a smelly oil heater in a safety cage. Condensation on all the windows. Wonky stairs to get into it. Grass, mud and snow trampled in. Only NQTs had classes in them – some kind of endurance test?
@HEPP_Jackie

The Lovely Head took me to one side at lunch and ended up telling me all about his money worries. I could see how it was troubling him. I told him it's ok to open up and I listened as intently as I could in a busy dining hall.

The Lovely Headteacher was really pleased to see me again! He shook my hand and virtually pulled me in from the double entrance doors. "Don't go anywhere!" he said, as he held me tightly.

"Geoff, I can't think straight. You're my only hope!"
"You've got this!" I say. I reassured him that I would go anywhere and cover as many classes as needed...
...and what a wonderful rounders tournament
we had!
Just me, four year groups and the site manager.

The Lovely Head is worried about staff morale. "It's taken a big hit during the pandemic, Geoff." He feels responsible.

"Keep doing what you're doing!" I said.
"Do your best for others and for the school
but be kind to yourself too! Remember,
morale is everybody's responsibility."

The Lovely Head has requested my service again today.
"We've children and staff off everywhere, and the SATs were delivered yesterday!" he sighed. I'm going in early.

Margaret will be back in the Year 1 class today:
"One more big push and I can sort everyone's pencil grip, Geoff!"

○   ⟲   ♡   ⬆

I've been in Year 5 today. I was next door to the Lovely Head, who took Year 6 himself. We caught up on playground duty.

"I don't mind teaching" he said, "but I still have a school to lead."

I helped a bit by covering his lunch duty.
"You'll need a break too" I said.
"Or you'll break."

○   ⟲   ♡   ⬆

Last week, the Lovely Head told me he has Imposter Syndrome. He feels like a fraud and is "waiting to be found out".

Many of us find it hard to accept our own accomplishments. We doubt ourselves.

I know exactly what this is.
It's not weakness.
It's humility.

○   ⟲   ♡   ⬆

Chapter Five: How We Used To Live (Part 2)

"Welcome to secondary school!
Your first piece of homework is to cover
your new exercise books in wallpaper…"

For a few days, Margaret has had her heart set on creating some mosaics with the class.

She couldn't decide whether to go with the Classical Roman style or the Vintage 1970s era.

Sadly, it turns out that gummed shapes aren't as easy to come by as they used to be.

The Penknife and The Pencil

I wonder if you remember doing this task, as a teacher?
Or perhaps, as a school child, you had a personalised pencil,
like this? (They didn't all say "Geoff".)

💬 ⇄ ♡ ⬆

Margaret just called.

"Do you remember the library bus, Geoff?" she asked.

"The driver was always traumatised from reversing in the big
car park and the steps to the bus were bigger than the infants'
legs. It was a lot of books and stress per square inch...
...a highlight of the term!"

💬 ⇄ ♡ ⬆

In the 1970s and 1980s, it was compulsory for all schools to employ at least one teacher who drove a Citroen 2CV.

That's not a guillotine!
This is a guillotine!

For today's lesson, Margaret will stamp your book and you'll just have to write a sentence and colour the picture.

B u s

jeep

S h i p

rocket

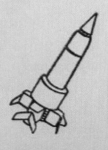

The Coomber:
Quintessential classroom
cassette player! It's
as heavy as a small
elephant. It looks like
it's from The Cold War.
But it sounds great (to
those whose headphones
work).

The BBC's Look and Read was the
longest running programme for
schools in the UK (1967-2004).

It featured the character Wordy
and stories including cult classics:
The Boy from Space (1971/1980)
Dark Towers (1981)
Badger Girl (1984)
Geordie Racer (1988)
Through the Dragon's Eye (1989)

Gather round, gather round!
Margaret is wheeling the big
TV in.

Everyone's invited!

But what schools programme
would you like to watch?

Topic Time:

Watching on the Big TV

What amazing times we live in! It's easy to take for granted the technology which has become part of our daily lives: at home, in the workplace and at school. Most of us have the internet at our fingertips – with the ability to search for almost anything in an instant. Children explore whole new worlds in virtual reality games. People of all ages can stream their favourite programmes and films, and watch them whenever they like. In education, from the EYFS to university, students use the latest technology to support their learning every single day.

But it wasn't always like this. There were simpler times.

We used to research information in encyclopaedias and libraries. As teachers, we illustrated our teaching points with chalk drawings on the blackboard and with posters that were stored in tubes. In school, it was a highlight of the week when the class listened to a radio programme (Time and Tune, anyone?).

But there was another highlight too. It's something which dates back to the late 1950s, when the BBC launched an innovative strand of educational programming. It's what generations of children fondly remember as "watching on the big TV".

Topic Time: Watching on the Big TV

By the 1970s, most primary schools had a big TV, and secondary schools typically had a few. The television sets seemed enormous. Compared to younger primary pupils, they probably were enormous! A typical school TV sat atop an unfeasibly cumbersome trolley and the TV trolley took real effort to manoeuvre around school. It was perhaps a Ferguson, a Panasonic or an Amstrad. By the mid-80s, some school TVs had a video and the posh ones even had a remote control. You couldn't stray too far with the remote though – it was attached to the TV on a cable.

Sometimes, a teacher would wheel the TV into their classroom at break time. The class would return from the playground and be elated that, for the next twenty minutes or so, they would be transported to another place. In primary schools, whole classes would huddle together on the floor and gasp in wonder at Wordie, Magic Grandad and The Boy from Space. They didn't mind straining their necks for this weekly highlight. In secondary schools, students tended to stay in their places. They could barely see the screen, but it made a lovely change from their regular teacher's voice.

By 1980, both the BBC and ITV were making around 50 series a year for schools and colleges. Meanwhile, some schools even had a designated TV room. Classes would be led to the TV room for the latest episode of whichever education series they were following. The trip to the TV room was an event in itself! Younger children saw the walk to the room as an adventure. Older children knew that walking slowly would take longer and therefore reduce lesson time either side of the TV programme. A particular highlight was when there was a live broadcast of a pioneering news event - perhaps a space mission or the raising of the Mary Rose.

You probably can't remember many specific handwriting lessons from your infancy but you can almost certainly remember Magic Pencil from Words and Pictures. You might not remember much about learning how to form numerals but, if you are of a certain age, you will undoubtedly remember the legend who was El Nombre! If you taught young children in the 1990s or if you attended school as a child at that time, you will probably have a special place in your heart for Aunt Mabel, her dog, Pippin, and their little, spotty aeroplane.

Old School Programmes on the Big TV

All Year Round	Music Time
Believe It or Not	Number Time (featuring El Nombre)
Biology	Outlook
Cats' Eyes	Out of the Past
Chemistry in Action	Over to You
Come Outside	Physics in Action
Discovery	Picture Box
Encounter	Primary Science
Experiment	Reading with Lenny
Facts for Life	Scene
Gather Round	Science All Around
Geography Today	Scientific Eye
Ghostwriter	Seeing and Doing
Going Places	Sing Together
Good Health	Song and Story
History Around You	Starting Out
How We Used to Live	Stop, Look and Listen
It's Fun to Read	Storytime
Just Look!	The Electric Company
Let's Read with Basil Brush	Thinkabout
Look and Read	Videomaths
Look Around	Vision On
Magic Grandad	Watch
Maths-in-a-Box	Words and Pictures
Merry-Go-Round	You and Me
Middle English	Zig Zag

Memories of Watching on the Big TV

You and Me and Geordie Racer!
Would you mind asking Margaret to pull
the shutters round it to stop the glare so we can count down
with the clock on BBC2?
@Fin75

💬   🔁   ♡   ↑

I spent the whole of my teaching career wheeling things
around; first a tall TV, then a BBC computer, then a trolley
laden with 20 laptops.
@LizanneLloyd

💬   🔁   ♡   ↑

Before I was a teacher, I chaired the parent group at my kids'
school. One day, the Headteacher rang and asked how much
cash we had – the big telly had gone to TV Heaven.
We were moving.
When we visited the new school, there were six TVs waiting for
testing in the corridor.
Therefore, a good school.
@EyesShutTeacher

💬   🔁   ♡   ↑

I wish BBC Schools would stream the catalogue of all their schools' programming. I'd love to have the "Watch" 1970s Christmas mini series, filmed in a cave in Bethlehem. I watched it as an infant, then taught with it 20 years later when I found a video in the back of a cupboard.
@wendyk101

We used to go into "the quiet room" (which later became "the quiet/noisy room") for this in P2/3 and I remember the teachers used to get cross if the class didn't settle quickly because when it started, it started and there was no "pause" button on the TV!
@Dawnf1

The children used to love Look and Read.

The days when English was fun! We took our class to Newcastle after watching Geordie Racer and they all cheered and clapped when they saw the Tyne Bridge!
@Sybellapiano

The Boy from Space terrified me!

Mum had to write a letter to excuse me from watching the last episode.

Even now, just looking at the picture, I feel the same!

@solly_bridget

This sounds mad but we watched a programme when I was small but I don't know what it was called. At the beginning, there was a black screen with a simplistic white clock made of white lozenges, rather than numbers. The hour hand moved round the screen and the lozenges disappeared.
@tomcatmam

Chapter Six: SATs Room 101

A Reflection:
Primary school assessments are going ahead "as normal" this summer. A six or seven year old in Year 2 is yet to experience a "normal" year in school. A child in Yr 6 last had an undisrupted year in Year 3. These aren't normal circumstances. We should invest more and test less.

💬   🔁   ♡   ⬆

The deputy head told Margaret about the Year 1 phonics test today. Margaret was the wrong person to talk to:
"What nonsense!" she said.
"Testing children by asking them to read words that aren't words!!
Learning to read is hard enough!"

Margaret was aghast, with a silent 'h'.

💬   🔁   ♡   ⬆

I caught up with Margaret earlier. I mentioned that I'd been in Year 6 today, boosting ahead of SATs.
"SATs are ridiculous, Geoff! They serve no useful purpose... I'm putting them in Room 101."

Margaret's School Room 101 also features The Literacy Hour, Kenneth Baker and Izal.

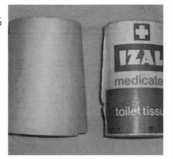

💬   🔁   ♡   ⬆

I was in Year 4 today but I caught up with The Lovely Head at the end of the day. He said he was proud of how calmly the Year 6 children approached the SPAG tests.
However, after a three year gap, he'd forgotten how stressful it is just putting the right tests in the right bags afterwards.

I've had two days in secondary so far this week. Exam season is upon us! Margaret and I send our best wishes to all Year 11 pupils as they begin their GCSEs. After all the uncertainty & disruption of the last two years, it's a commendable achievement simply to reach this point!

I was back in primary today and caught up with the Lovely Head. He's worried about SATs results day tomorrow. He hasn't been sleeping well: "I haven't missed this feeling over the last two years!" he said. It's no good me telling a worrier not to worry so I just listened.

Chapter Seven: Pumps, Plimsolls and Bear Feet

Margaret had to think on her feet today.
The Year 2 PE plan simply said "Big Apparatus".
Most of the lesson was spent getting the apparatus out, going over safety rules and putting it all away again.
But the children loved the climbing and jumping.
All fifteen minutes of it...

💬   ⟲   ♡   ⬆

Margaret is tired after doing PE with Year 1 today.
"I was run ragged, Geoff!"
Margaret says she'd forgotten that getting changed is a lesson in itself.
She'd also forgotten that there's nothing simple about the instructions
"Line up!"
"Find a space!" or
"Hold your balls still!"

💬   ⟲   ♡   ⬆

Margaret was surprised to learn that today's school takes part in The Daily Mile: "I've never run a mile in my life, Geoff!"

It's not how Margaret would have chosen to "wear in" her brand new shoes but she did enjoy the brisk walk.

She also finished first in her age category.

Well today's mixed-age class was delightful!
I'm not entirely sure who was Year 3 and who was Year 4 but I'm not even sure it matters. What is age anyway?
The highlight of the day was PE with the large apparatus!
At playtime, one of the children drew the lesson we'd just had.

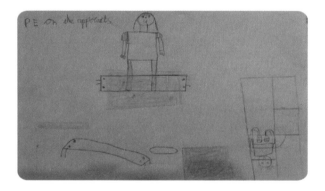

Well today's secondary kept me on my toes!
"Can you cover PE?" the deputy asked on my arrival.
She had perhaps expected a slightly younger supply teacher.
"Why not?" I replied.

And what a day we had.
Crab football all the way!

There will be some tired arms and legs tomorrow...

💬   ↻   ♡   ⬆

Margaret's had a tiring day in Reception.

She's a big fan of the EYFS Areas of Learning but she's decided there's one key area missing.

Margaret says it's a matter which takes up a considerable part of the school day, every day.

It's called "Getting ready for hometime, Geoff!"

💬   ↻   ♡   ⬆

BBC Radio – Movement & Music, Stage One

Live programmes twice a week.
No P.E. kit? No problem!

You'll be absolutely fine in your vest, pants and bare feet.

💬   ↻   ♡   ⬆

Movement and Music
Stage One

Age 5–6 Wednesday 11.20–11.40 Thursday 9.55–10.15 (not N. Ireland)
This series broadcast by Penny Whittam   Produced by Vera Gray

Cowboy's dance

Margaret asked Doris to collect the equipment from the PE store.

When Doris eventually returned, she was fuming about filthy beanbags, missing quoits and tangled team bands.

Neither Margaret nor Doris felt like practising for sports day but the PE store is much tidier now.

◯   ⇄   ♡   ⬆

In this morning's English lesson, Margaret taught Year 2 about homophones.

In P.E. this afternoon, some of the children had forgotten their plimsolls. They ended up joining in with bear feet.

Margaret will go over homophones tomorrow.

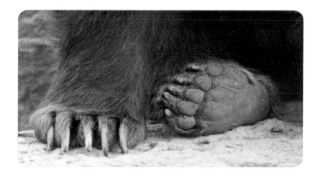

◯   ⇄   ♡   ⬆

TOPIC TIME: SCHOOL TRIPS

For all the several thousand days you spent in school as a child, it was the relatively small number of days you spent out of school which will have given you some of your most vivid memories. We're talking about coaches. We're talking about egg sandwiches, Tupperware containers, back-packs and and pac-a-macs. We're talking about sick buckets, paper towels and the excitement of stopping at a service station for a toilet break ("Welcome to South Mimms!"). We're talking about mythical tales of young children smuggling penguins home from the zoo. We're talking, of course, about the school trip!

The school trip has been an enjoyable and invaluable aspect of school life for generations of children. It's been something to look forward to and something to write about afterwards! From the youngest pupils going on walks in their locality to the oldest students going on foreign expeditions, from the farm to the seaside, from pantomimes to Shakespearean plays, from an hour in the town library to a few days on a residential - the trip has something for everyone. The trip could brighten any time of the school year too, though it's perhaps summer term excursions that are the most fondly remembered. If your school trip destination was a theme park (Wicksteed Park, anyone? The American Adventure?), it was basically like winning the lottery!

Topic Time: School Trips

Perhaps you visited a castle or a mill as part of a history topic? Maybe you experienced some role play in a Victorian classroom at Beamish or Wigan Pier? Perhaps your curriculum topic led you to Jodrell Bank Observatory, to the Jorvik Viking Centre or to the Lake District? Sometimes, it wasn't the purpose of the trip that excited children the most though. It wasn't always even the destination. It was the anticipation! What will I wear? Who will I sit next to on the coach? Will the bus be a double-decker? Will my mum be a parent helper? Will the teacher be wearing their own clothes too? What time will lunch be?

Of course, if you're reading this as a teacher, the words "school trip" might not initially evoke feelings of warm nostalgia. Instead, they might cause palpitations! After all, trips could be stressful to plan and intense to supervise/lead. There was the challenge of getting all the permission slips in. (So simple and yet so hard.) Then there was the matter of collecting the money. There was always plenty of paperwork, even before risk assessments became more complex than the trip itself. Let's be honest though, logistics aside, the school trip is pretty good for everybody. A trip is a change from the classroom, for pupils and school staff alike. It's about hands-on learning, socialising and discovery. The school trip is a chance for pupils to relax a little, away from the usual routines and pressures. Dare I say it? Trips are even about having fun!

Part of the magic of the school trip lies in the fact that trips can provide opportunities for all sorts of "firsts". Residential trips have given generations of children their first overnight stay away from home, their first experience of outdoor pursuits or their first trip abroad. Day trips have provided new opportunities too. Perhaps it's the awe of entering a cave, the wonder of walking on a beach or the pleasure of sitting in a theatre seat. There's also the excitement of using a particular mode of transport for the first time: a bus; a train; a ferry or even a plane! Then there are the animals! Most primary school careers include a trip to a farm, a zoo or a safari park. For some children – more than we might expect – these occasions offer the very first glimpse of animals in real life. The joy Is priceless.

"Look!! A cow!!" shouted the Reception child, filled with excitement, pointing at a horse.

Memories of School Trips

Best trip ever...went to Blackpool Airport and flew back over our school in Downham, Lancashire. One of the leavers had a dad who was a pilot!

Imagine the risk assessment this would need now!!
@kirsteen1972

We used to go to Alton Towers from Carlisle.
The bus dropped us off and then picked us up later in the day. Never saw a teacher the whole day, no mobile phones or safety procedures. You knew if you didn't get back on the bus at the end of the day, you'd be left!
@holliesca5

We went to Whipsnade in about 1972. The coach home was delayed whilst the HT counted and recounted.

Someone was missing. The zoo was searched.

Eventually a register was found.

Everyone was there. The mystery was solved when the HT realised she had forgotten to count herself.

@lawzthemase

○   ⇄   ♡   ⬆

Residentials are always fun. Ish.

There's the:

-child who brings ALL THE CHOCOLATES!

-child who brings enough clothes to last a month. It's for two days!

-unique smell of a dorm at 6am. (Or whenever rise and shine is.)

-the REALLY HAPPY instructor.

How do they do it?

@thursnextus

○   ⇄   ♡   ⬆

Staffing my first school trip, Year 8 going to France in 2007. Clearing up rubbish and one child throws a camera in the bin bag. They said it was a disposable one and they'd taken all the pictures...

@smurfomatic

○   ⇄   ♡   ⬆

25+ year ago....Forty or so infants going on a steam train trip –
arrived at the station, which was run by volunteers, just in time
for the train's imminent departure.
Children overly excited, jostling on the platform, so
I blew my whistle - and the train promptly left without us!
@Mrs__EM

Y10 PRU students seeing penguins and amazed that they were
a real animal. Magical!
@MrsGtweets20

Travelling across Germany
in 1983, with just two
cassettes on the coach:

Queen's Greatest Hits and
Now That's What I Call
Music 2.

To this day, I know all the
words to all the songs!
@thealistairw

Chapter 8: The End of Year Assembly

Margaret and I are delighted to announce that we will be rounding off this school year with our very own End of Year Assembly.

The Lovely Head is again loaning us the old school piano and his hymn folder, with acetates which were once in alphabetical order.

○   ⟲   ♡   ⬆

I have been passing on all your school hymn requests to Margaret, for her assembly planning.

Margaret has asked me to point out that, if you were one of the children who used to sing "I am the Lord of the Dance settee", then you are confusing theology and Sofology.

○   ⟲   ♡   ⬆

Thanks to the hot weather and some school closures, Margaret and I ended up with an unexpected free day! We met up over Zoom to plan our End of Year Assembly.

Margaret isn't great with technology though:
"I would have preferred a Zoom lolly or Zoom by Fat Larry's Band, Geoff!"

$\bigcirc$ ♻   ♡   ⬆

21 Jul 22

It's time for Geoff and Margaret's first
(and possibly last)
End of Year Assembly!

Margaret has just run a few more copies of the programme through the Banda.

**Geoff and Margaret's
END OF YEAR
ASSEMBLY**
Thursday 21st July, 2022
7.30pm
@RetirementTales

Everybody sit up straight and face the front!

Let us begin...

$\bigcirc$ ♻   ♡   ⬆

Geoff and Margaret's End of Year Assembly
@RetirementTales
Thursday 21st July, at 7.30pm

Entry Music - Count On Me by Bruno Mars

1. Welcome

2. Song - Colours of Day (Light Up The Fire)

3. Year 6 Pupils' Memories

4. Song - Lord of the Dance

5. The Vicar

6. Song - Father, We Adore You (sung in a round)

7. Poem - You Are My Favourite Teacher

8. Song - Who Put the Colours in the Rainbow?

9. Year 6 Pupils and School Recorder Club - Memories by Maroon 5

10. Staff Goodbyes/Presentation

11. Song - One More Step Along the World I Go

12. Presentation to Year 6 Leavers (Hall of Fame)

13. Summer Safety Notices

Exit Music - Lord, Dismiss Us With Thy Blessing

The end of term
and the end of part two

PART THREE:
THE AUTUMN TERM

"Teaching is the one profession that creates all other professions."

- Unknown source

PART THREE:
THE AUTUMN TERM

Chapter One: A New School Year

31 Aug 22

On the eve of a new school year, Margaret and I send our thanks and best wishes to everyone working in childcare and education.

Sure, it's a tough draw but it's still a privilege to work with children and young people. Amongst the politics and the bureaucracy, your gift is to shape lives.

◯   ⟲   ♡   ↥

Geoff and Margaret's September Staff INSET (Baker Day):

Breakfast Rolls
1. A Positive Mindset
Coffee and El Nombre
2. Geoff's Pop Quiz
Pub Lunch
3. Early Reading
Tea and Biscuits, and Granny's Garden
4. Margaret's TV Detectives
Early Finish

◯   ⟲   ♡   ↥

Apologies if anybody feels our INSET day is thin on pedagogy. Margaret says she could do something on Piaget's theory of cognitive development but then there would be less time on Cagney and Lacey.

◯   ⟲   ♡   ↥

The agency has called...

...our work resumes on Tuesday.

I've polished the Hush Puppies again.

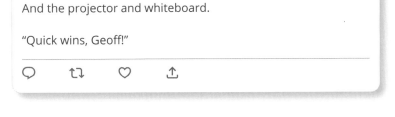

$\bigcirc$ ⇄ ♡ ↥

Margaret is all ready for school tomorrow!
She's covering a mixed Year One/Two class all day.

The agency has actually offered Margaret a full week but she's
going to see how tomorrow goes before she commits.

Besides, she could be the new Education Secretary by
Wednesday.

$\bigcirc$ ⇄ ♡ ↥

The new sign on the Year One/Two classroom door said:
"Save electricity! Save money!"

Margaret didn't need telling twice.
She left the computer off all day.
And the projector and whiteboard.

"Quick wins, Geoff!"

$\bigcirc$ ⇄ ♡ ↥

Margaret's been in Year 1 today She was delighted to see a piano in the hall and even more delighted to find some classic books in the cupboard. Margaret couldn't make much sense of the maths or the phonics plan but the music needed no planning at all.

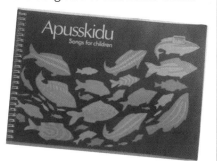

"A day of highs and lows!"

♡ ⇄ ♡ ⬆

Margaret has had another good day in Reception and she's even found a new friend in the deputy head;
"She's lovely, Geoff! And so young!"

Margaret asked the deputy how old she is.
"28" the deputy replied.
"28?!" Margaret exclaimed.
"I've got turtle necks older than you!"

♡ ⇄ ♡ ⬆

Margaret is feeling a bit brighter after a very busy morning in a nursery class: "They kept me on my toes, Geoff!"

She had 12 children who started last week, 6 new children who started today and one young man who, it turned out, should have been in Reception.

♡ ⇄ ♡ ⬆

Margaret has been covering classes while teachers had their appraisal review meetings today. She was in Year 2 first, then Reception and then Year 1. "I've been up and down like a yo-yo, Geoff!"

Margaret has never been a big fan of performance management. You can't measure "maverick".

💬   🔁   ♡   ⬆️

Margaret couldn't resist the piano in the hall today; she spent the first part of lunchtime tinkling the ivories. The children and midday staff were very impressed!

One of the Reception boys also had a little tinkle in the hall but that was met with less positivity overall.

💬   🔁   ♡   ⬆️

Margaret has taught a full week in Reception.

She thinks she might need a lie down in a dark room. Or perhaps to hibernate until the spring.

💬   🔁   ♡   ⬆️

Chapter Two: Autumn Days
(When the Grass is Jewelled)

Margaret has been in Reception again today.

One of the boys really didn't want to go into class this morning. At the end of the day, the same boy didn't want to go home! "All in a day's work!" said Margaret, modestly.

Here's to Reception teachers and their unique skills/magical powers!

Margaret has taken a few liberties today.
She felt the Reception classroom was lacking "a certain something". That certain something was an autumn display.

Margaret took the children on a walk around the school grounds this afternoon.

The display will be up by the weekend!

The agency called earlier.
Margaret has been requested by the same school as last week, for the same Reception class.
Margaret hopes the regular teacher is ok but she is rather chuffed to be going back. She has a nature table to put together and an autumn display to finish.

Whether you're talking about Hairy Hat Man, He-Man or H from Steps, Margaret would like to remind everybody that this letter name is pronounced "aitch" not "haitch".

Margaret was in Year 2 again today.
The timetable for the morning said:
Assembly;
Phonics;
English;
Times Tables;
Maths;
Guided Reading;
SPAG and Handwriting.

Margaret thinks we ask a lot of young children these days. "There's hardly room for playtime."

It's here:
The "Autumn Days" T-shirt!
Including:
Jet planes meeting in the air
to be refuelled;
Clouds that look like familiar faces;
Swallows curving in the sky and
many more!

Autumn Days

When the grass
is jewelled...

♡   ⊔⊐   ♡   ⬆

Margaret taught Year 2 this afternoon.
History was on the timetable.
"Are you OK teaching about The Great Fire of London?" the
deputy asked.

Margaret has been OK teaching about The Great Fire of London
since the National Curriculum was invented in 1988.

♡   ⊔⊐   ♡   ⬆

Chapter Three:
Assembly Time – Come & Praise!

Margaret was in Year 2 today.
She forgot to take the class into the vicar's mid-morning assembly. A child came to remind Margaret but Margaret decided it was too late by then.

"I did my own collective worship in class later on."

Praise the Lord for Margaret's Ladybird books!

💬   🔁   ♡   ⬆️

The sound system wouldn't work in assembly today. Margaret saw the deputy was getting quite stressed so she decided to give a helping hand.

The piano wasn't really in tune and nobody knew the song but Margaret went for it anyway.

By breaktime, everyone was singing Lord, Kum ba Yah.

💬   🔁   ♡   ⬆️

Margaret taught music today, using one of her favourite school hymn books: "Their Words, My Thoughts". She's had it since the school first gave them to pupils and staff in 1982.

Margaret has always enjoyed hymn #5: Father, We Adore You.

Sung in a three part round, this was a staple of Margaret's assemblies and music lessons through the 80s and 90s.

It undoubtedly influenced lots of children's views of religion (...and music lessons...and assemblies).

We're trying to track down the Come and Praise kids!

Last seen in 1978. Where are they now?

Margaret thinks these boys might be Gary, Robbie, Mark, Howard and Jason.

I think she's confusing Relight My Fire and Light Up the Fire (Song 55).

Here's a very special collection!
The songs you sang.
The songs you hummed.
The songs you played on the recorder.
The songs you read from the over-head projector.
The songs you loved and the songs you loathed.
The songs that brought you together!

This week's old school hymn is "When I Needed a Neighbour".

Please turn to song 65 in your Come & Praise books and please do not smirk or giggle at the third verse.

The song has a serious message and the lyrics have never been more important.

1 When I needed a neighbour, were you there,
   were you there?
   When I needed a neighbour, were you there?

Chorus:
And the creed and the colour and the name
won't matter,
Were you there?

2 I was hungry and thirsty, were you there,
   were you there?
   I was hungry and thirsty, were you there?
   Chorus

3 I was cold, I was naked, were you there,
   were you there?
   I was cold, I was naked, were you there?
   Chorus

4 When I needed a shelter, were you there,
   were you there?
   When I needed a shelter, were you there?
   Chorus

5 When I needed a healer, were you there,
   were you there?
   When I needed a healer, were you there?
   Chorus

6 Wherever you travel, I'll be there, I'll be there,
   Wherever you travel, I'll be there.

Chorus:
And the creed and the colour and the name
won't matter,
I'll be there.

                                    Sydney Carter

TOPIC TIME

The **Come and Praise** Hymn Book

Here's some food for thought! Between your first day in primary school and your last day in secondary school, you probably attended somewhere between one thousand and two thousand assemblies. Remember everyone being in the hall together? It was a squash, wasn't it? In primary school, you had to sit cross-legged on the floor. That parquet flooring was cold. If you were in a certain class or year group, you might occasionally have been allowed to sit on a wooden PE bench – what a privilege! In the summer term, the hall was stifling and there was always someone prone to fainting. If a bee or wasp made it into an assembly, there could be pandemonium. In secondary school, you might have been expected to stand for the whole assembly. They were sometimes very long. There were sometimes school hymns in Latin. There was more fainting.

Now, you probably won't remember very much about what was said at all those assemblies you sat through but, one thing's for certain, you'll remember what you sang! You'll remember what you sang because you sang it often. You sang with your friends and your class and your school. Sometimes, you sang loudly. Sometimes, you hummed. Sometimes, you sang the wrong words on purpose (Cue: "I am the Lord of the damp settee") and sometimes the words were upside down. Sometimes you sang in a round and sometimes you sang as you left the hall. You often sang songs without even thinking what the words meant, but the singing brought the school together.

When you think back to all those assemblies, there will be certain images that spring to mind: the hall curtains; the overhead projector and the upright piano, amongst others. If you were lucky enough to be an Assembly Monitor, you might recall the lever arch file of acetates, some of which were in alphabetical order. For a long time, there was another assembly staple too – the hymn book.

Topic Time: The "Come & Praise" School Hymn Book

In 1978, the BBC published a collection of hymns for schools. Other hymn books existed too, but this one was different. It had a two-tone blue front cover, featuring the faces of five, floppy-haired young children. On the inside, the book featured 72 songs which went on to be sung in schools around the country and which made their way into the nation's psyche. That book was called "Come and Praise". It was compiled by Geoffrey Marshall-Taylor, a man who had been tasked with bringing together the best and most popular songs from the Radio Department of BBC School Broadcasting.

As well as compiling songs which were already well-known in assemblies around the land, Come and Praise also included a number of new compositions. These songs were Christian but the themes were often universal, meaning the tunes were belted out in Church schools and community schools alike. If you are lucky enough to still own a copy of the original Come and Praise book (it's quite a collector's item!), you'll see that it reads like the tracklisting of Now That's What I Call an Assembly! From Water of Life, with its busy workman digging in the desert, to Autumn Days, with jet planes meeting in the air to be refuelled. From songs about the created world (Who Put the Colours in the Rainbow?) to songs about the journey of life (One More Step), the hymns were melodic and accessible. As Geoffrey Marshall-Taylor noted in the introduction to the book, "Above all, my belief is that songs in assembly should be enjoyed, not endured."

In 2021 and 2022, comedian Jason Manford performed a mammoth stand-up tour of the UK, with a show called "Like Me". Each show included a nostalgic piece about school assembly songs and each night ended with a mass singalong: When I Needed a Neighbour...Lord of the Dance... Give Me Oil in My Lamp...By the end of the tour, entire arenas were filled with the familiar verses and choruses last sung in school halls. It was euphoric. The music was still universal. An "Assembly Bangers" medley was released in response to popular demand. An album followed too, with cover art paying homage to a certain school hymn book. It turns out those assembly songs were enjoyed by a great many. They endured too.

Old School Assembly Hymns

All Things Bright and Beautiful

At Half Past Three We Go Home to Tea

Autumn Days

Black and White

Calon Lân

Cauliflowers Fluffy

Colours of Day (Light Up the Fire)

Cross Over the Road

Father, We Adore You

For Those in Peril on the Sea

From the Tiny Ant

Give Me Oil In My Lamp

Go Tell It on the Mountain

Have You Heard the Raindrops (Water of Life)

He Who Would Valiant Be

He's Got the Whole World in His Hands

I Have Seen the Golden Sunshine

I The Lord of Sea and Sky (Here I am Lord)

If I Had a Hammer

If I Were a Butterfly

Jerusalem

Jesus' Love is Very Wonderful

Kum Ba Yah

Lord, Dismiss Us with Thy Blessing

Lord of the Dance

Magic Penny (Love is Something if You Give it Away)

Old School Assembly Hymns

Morning Has Broken

My God is So Big

One More Step Along the World I Go

Onward Christian Soldiers

Peace, Perfect Peace

Praise Him

Rise and Shine

Shine Jesus Shine

Streets of London

Thank You, Lord

The Best Gift (I Will Bring to You)

The Lord's Prayer

The Wise Man Built his House upon the Rock

There is a Green Hill Far Away

Think of a World Without Any Flowers

This Little Light of Mine

Water of Life

We Plough the Fields and Scatter

When a Knight Won his Spurs

When I Needed a Neighbour

Who Built the Ark?

Who Put the Colours in the Rainbow?

Wide, Wide as the Ocean

Will Your Anchor Hold in the Storms of Life?

Zaccheus Was a Very Little Man

There's been a lot of painting today in Reception. Margaret says the children were pretty good at helping themselves to the ready-mix!

She recalls that, in her first school, even the staff had to serve an apprenticeship before they were allowed anywhere near the powder paint.

Here's a 1970s blackboard rubber/ projectile missile.

These could rub out at a speed of five words per second and travel from the front to the back of the classroom in two seconds flat.

Chances are, if you were a child of the 70s or 80s, this was the first school desk you ever sat at!

Margaret is exasperated.

It took half the lesson just to find the keys to the iPad trolley and the other half for everybody to log on.

Margaret remembers when ICT was one computer, two children at a time, a weekly tick-list and the choice of Paint or Granny's Garden.

Margaret says she has had a lovely day but she was exhausted by lunchtime and so were the children.

When Margaret is Education Secretary, she's going to mandate afternoon power naps for children and staff.

"Everybody put your head on your desk...!

○   ⇄   ♡   ↥

Margaret's top tip for setting up your classroom is to re-use everyday household items for storage.

"It's better for the environment and better for your pocket, Geoff!"

○   ⇄   ♡   ↥

Margaret used to really enjoy taking the tub of wooden letter templates home, ready for a weekend of drawing and cutting out for her latest display.

After she'd sorted out the title, Margaret could then get on with all the mounting.

○   ⇄   ♡   ↥

Depending on your age, you either remember stamping coins in children's books as a teacher or colouring, labelling and adding them together as an infant.

For anybody who is really young, coins are how we used to pay for things.

Please open your geography exercise books on the next blank page. I'll be coming around the classroom and rolling out a map of Great Britain in everybody's books...

Read, Write, Think!

60 years ago, James Pitman invented the Initial Teaching Alphabet – i.t.a. (there were no capitals!).

It was intended to be a practical, simplified writing system but many children struggled to transfer their i.t.a. reading skills to reading standard English.

Consonants

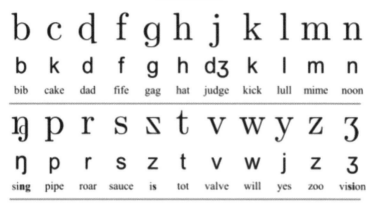

b	c	d̡	f	g	h	j	k	l	m	n
b	k	d	f	g	h	dʒ	k	l	m	n
bib	cake	dad	fife	gag	hat	judge	kick	lull	mime	noon

ŋ	p	r	s	ꭥ	t	v	w	y	z	ʒ
ŋ	p	r	s	z	t	v	w	j	z	ʒ
sing	pipe	roar	sauce	is	tot	valve	will	yes	zoo	vision

Joined consonants   Short vowels

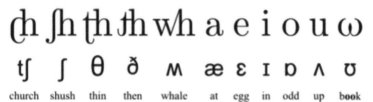

c̡h	ʃh	t̡h	f̡h	wh	a	e	i	o	u	ꭥ
tʃ	ʃ	θ	ð	ʍ	æ	ɛ	ɪ	ɒ	ʌ	ʊ
church	shush	thin	then	whale	at	egg	in	odd	up	book

Long vowels / diphthongs

uɒ	æ	au	ɛɛ	œ	ꭥ	ue	ie	ɔi	ou
ɑː	eɪ	ɔː	iː	oʊ	uː	juː	aɪ	ɔɪ	aʊ
father	ape	all	eat	oak	ooze	use	ice	oil	owl

Also, **𝒓** is used following a vowel letter to write the sound in "earn" etc

120

TOPIC TIME: READING SCHEMES

Here are some boys: John; Peter; Ben and Kipper.
Here are some girls: Janet; Jane; Jennifer Yellow-hat and Biff.
Here are some dogs: Tip; Pat; Lad and Floppy.
Here are some reading schemes!

Reading schemes have been a staple of primary education and an integral part of the process of learning to read for generations. Whether you were brought up with Janet and John in the 1950s or Kipper and Floppy in the 1990s, you will have had a similar experience of learning to read. Remember reading your book to your teacher, perhaps at their desk, in a queue or in a group? Remember the key word flashcards, rehearsed in class every day and practised again at home every evening? Remember how it felt when you were allowed to change your own reading book? The pride! Whatever your age, you probably even remember where you had to go to get a new book. Were your class's reading scheme books just kept on a shelf or were they organised neatly into ice-cream tubs? There have always been a lot of ice cream tubs in our schools.

There have been a great many reading schemes adopted by UK schools over the last 75 years. Sometimes, particular schemes were used for many, many years only to suddenly fall out of favour or fashion. Sometimes, particular schemes have been loved by some children, teachers and schools, whilst being simultaneously loathed by others.

You can't please everyone though! Here is a brief overview of just a few of the reading schemes which have been used the most prolifically in the last seventy years. Whatever your memories and whatever your views, it's true to say that these four schemes alone helped millions of children learn to read.

One Two Three and Away!
(The Village with Three Corners)

The reading scheme "One Two Three and Away!" was written by Sheila K. McCullagh and first published by Collins in the late 1960s. Those who were brought up reading these books also refer to the scheme as "The Village with Three Corners" (the setting of the stories) or sometimes as "Jennifer Yellow-hat" or "Roger Red-hat" (two of the main characters from the series). The scheme gained popularity through the 1970s and the books were reprinted regularly until the 1990s.

More than fifty years after publication, it's fair to say that this particular reading scheme has achieved a kind of cult status. Copies of books about Jennifer Yellow-hat and her friends are highly sought after. Small world figures of the characters were once a common resource in infant classrooms; they can now fetch almost £100 on eBay. For reference, when these books were first published, a teacher would have earned around £150 a month!

Sheila K. McCullagh also wrote a number of series for more advanced readers, including the fondly remembered Griffin Pirate Stories (1959), Dragon Pirate Stories (1964) and Tim and the Hidden People (1974). In the 1980s, McCullagh went on to pen a collection of stories which were animated for the YTV programme, Puddle Lane – a series aimed at pre-school children and which was later published by Ladybird Books.

Eventually, "One Two Three and Away!" fell out of fashion and the scheme made way for others which were phonetically decodeable. However, this story doesn't end there. In recent years, the rights to this reading scheme were acquired by a dedicated fan, the books have been republished by The Reading Hut Ltd and the stories now form part of a project called "I Can Read Without You". As if that's not enough cause for celebration, there is a "Village with Three Corners Appreciation Society" on Facebook...

Janet and John

The Janet and John book series (not to be confused with Terry Wogan's Janet and John audio series) will be very familiar to the generations who attended infant classes during the 1950s, 60s and early 70s. According to The Oxford Companion to Children's Literature (Carpenter and Prichard, 1984), this reading scheme was used by 81% of British primary schools by 1968. In the mid-1970s, the books fell out of favour, for reasons relating both to the design of the stories and the overall approach to the teaching of reading. However, for more than a quarter of a century, most of the nation's school children learned to read with Janet and John.

The stories of siblings Janet and John are often remembered as being quintessentially middle class and English. In actual fact, this reading scheme has American origins. The tales of Janet and John were based on a series called Alice and Jerry (A.K.A. The Reading Foundation Series), written by Mabel O'Donnell and first published in the USA in the 1940s by Row, Peterson and Company. Janet and John were born in the UK in 1949, after publisher James Nisbet & Co acquired the licence to republish the Alice and Jerry series under a new name. The books, redesigned for young British readers, credit both the original American author and former teacher, Roma Munro, who had been tasked with Anglicising the text. Janet and John quickly became a popular reading scheme here in the UK, mirroring the success of Alice and Jerry in schools across the USA.

If you grew up with Janet and John, you'll recall that this scheme used the "look and say" approach to reading. Words were repeated regularly, helping children to memorise them. If you enjoyed the stories, you might credit this repetition with having helped you to become a reader. If you didn't like the stories, you might credit this repetition with having turned you off reading.

It's almost 75 years since stories of Janet and John made their way onto British shores and into British schools. Times might have changed and the scheme has long since disappeared from the classroom. But the books have retained a certain charm and there is a successful marketplace for vintage copies of the original books and for special editions which continue to be printed today.

If you want to be transported back to simpler times, pick up an old Janet and John story, flick through a few pages and admire the charming illustrations. You'll pick up the words soon enough. If you like your stories to have a little less repetition and a bit more innuendo, you might prefer the Terry Wogan versions.

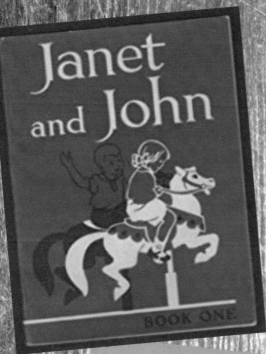

The Ladybird Key Words Reading Scheme, with Peter and Jane

The Key Words Reading Scheme was devised by headmaster William Murray and first published by Ladybird in 1964. Although other reading schemes were in common use by the mid-60s, this was the first series of its kind in UK schools. As the name suggests, this particular scheme was based on key words – those which occur the most frequently in the English language. The Ladybird reading books introduced new words gradually and repeated them frequently. Children learned to read words on sight, using the "Look and Say" approach. It was a simple and successful model! The overall structure of the Ladybird scheme was relatively straightforward too. There were twelve levels of book, with three books at each level (a, b and c). The first book in each level introduced young readers to new words. The second book provided practice at reading those words in different contexts. The third book encouraged children to practise writing the words they were learning, whilst also introducing the use of phonics.

As I write this book, it's fair to say that the teaching of early reading continues to be a topic of some contention. In particular, threads about phonics seem to be amongst the most fiery of all topics on EduTwitter. Far be it from me to wade into debates about pedagogy though. I'll just say that it's not a new debate. Here's what the Key Words creator had to say about the matter, in 1964:

"English is not a purely phonetic language, so care must be taken in presenting this method to the learner. Too much emphasis on the phonetic method, especially if used too early in the programme, can slow down progress and harm the attitude towards reading." (William Murray)

The story of Ladybird's Key Words reading scheme is perhaps the most remarkable of all the Ladybird stories. First published in 1964, books remain in publication almost sixty years later. Perhaps it was the illustrations. Perhaps it was the simplicity. Either way, it's not just nostalgia. The Key Words Reading Scheme found its way into the nation's classrooms and the books found their way into children's bedrooms and hearts. Books about Peter, Jane and Pat, the dog, went on to sell almost 100 million copies around the world. William Murray's work changed the way we approached literacy.

Has there EVER been any other educational resource with such longevity and impact?

1c Read and write

The Ladybird Key Words
Reading Scheme

The Oxford Reading Tree

The Oxford Reading Tree was created by author Roderick Hunt and first published by the Oxford University Press in 1986. The scheme, largely illustrated by Alex Brychta, started out as a series of thirty stories, all about a young boy, Kipper, his siblings, Biff and Chip, and their family antics. Mum and Dad featured heavily too, as did Floppy the dog. All good reading schemes need a dog.

The premise of the Oxford Reading Tree was simple and not dissimilar to its forerunners. Young readers were introduced to a family of characters and a small number of new words at a time. The stories were simple yet relatable; the illustrations were filled with humour and talking points. With this particular scheme, children were encouraged to use a range of strategies to read the books. They learned some words on sight, decoded others phonetically and used picture cues as prompts.

Roderick Hunt's book scheme might have started out as a modest tree but it quickly grew in scale and popularity. The books established themselves as the reading scheme of choice and it's said that, at one time, the Oxford Reading Tree was used in 80% of the nation's primary schools. They were used by schools in 120 other countries too! Hunt and Brychta kept the interest going by writing and illustrating prolifically. The series eventually evolved to include non-fiction books and poetry. Other authors and illustrators were brought in too, adding variety. Julia Donaldson contributed the Songbirds series. Over the years, the scheme grew to include more than 800 books. It's a wonder they never renamed it the Oxford Reading Forest.

Millions of children have learned to read with Biff, Chip and Kipper over the last four decades. They will remember taking their reading book home, perhaps with a set of key word flashcards to learn. The process of learning to read was supported by an expansive array of teaching resources. There were big books of each story, workbooks and ink stampers. There were audio cassettes, board games and CD ROMS (remember them?). At home, children could watch the animated programme The Magic Key (2000) on Cbeebies and - two decades later - live-action stories of Biff and Chip (2021) on CBBC.

Back in the classroom, some young children read The Toys' Party, then took great delight at following the recipe for Kipper's cake. They put in cornflakes. They put in baked beans. They put in sugar. They made a right mess. They enjoyed the reading and the role play. Some of those children are teachers now too.

The Toys' Party

Roderick Hunt   Alex Brychta

Chapter Five: Banished but Bouncing Back!

On November 2nd, 2022, Twitter determined that Retirement Tales had broken the rules.

Alas, there had been too much joy and mild peril. The account was permanently suspended.

The news was shared by our good friends @HeadteacherChat:

We have received the following message
from Geoff and Margaret @RetirementTales:

"I am very sorry to say that Margaret and
I have been permanently excluded from
Twitter over night.
We hope to be back.
If this is the end of The Call, thank you
for everything."

#Hope

The Fall Out!

We have been through so much – Geoff and Margaret have got
us through a pandemic, budget cuts, multiple policy changes
and education secretaries, an energy crisis, a cost of living crisis,
a recruitment crisis...this is terrible news.

@Head-ful-dreams

Maybe that's the reason – Geoff and Margaret have been making waves by encouraging us to realise we're more powerful than we've been led to believe.
@oadbyfsf

💬   🔁   ♡   ⬆️

Oh my! Is Apuskidu a swear word now or something?
Or is a waterfall cardigan a euphemism for something illegal?
@thepetitioner

💬   🔁   ♡   ⬆️

When things seemed black and bleak, Geoff and Margaret were always there with their rainbow views of the world of teaching and the world in general.
Thank you, Retirement Tales!
@ellerhowhouse

💬   🔁   ♡   ⬆️

Look who's trending!
@AmandaM33106612

Television · Last night
Question Time

Trending in United Kingdom
Sacked
17.9K Tweets

Trending in United Kingdom
#freeGeoffandMargaret

💬   🔁   ♡   ⬆️

A New Account !

03 Nov 22

We got knocked down
But we got up again.
You're never gonna keep us down.

Margaret says that's the last time she
ever takes a Tesla for a joyride.

GeoffandMargaretToo@RetirementTale5

We are back! But who knows how long for?
Please read our full message next!

The End of Retirement Tales?

I'm very sorry to say that Margaret and I have been permanently suspended from our first Twitter account. We weren't ready to say "goodbye" but we might not be allowed on Twitter anymore. We have sadly lost our community of thirty-five thousand followers and almost a year's worth of Tweets and memories. If we get censored here too, please read this thread and share it as widely and quickly as possible.

When Margaret and I answered "The Call" at the start of January, we didn't have a plan. We simply wanted to help. We had no idea what lay ahead in schools nor how we would grow a very special community here on Twitter.

It quickly became apparent to us that schools and the education system were in something of a crisis in a world changed by the pandemic. We pledged to stay around until the wind changed. Our hope was to support you, to put our arms around you, metaphorically, and to keep you buoyant.

It's been a pleasure to have spent the last year with you. You have been good friends to us and we hope we have been good friends to you. The wind never did change really. It still blows fiercely, just in different directions now.

This world can be dark, segregated and judgemental. Educationalists can disagree fervently and social media can be a mean and toxic space. 'Retirement Tales' has been about light, unity and good old-fashioned fun. Our little Twitter account has simply been about bringing joy and hope: the best of things.

Margaret and I believe in children and young people. We believe in schools and education. We believe that teaching is a vocation and a privilege (despite the many challenges). We believe that teachers can change a child's world. Without teachers, support staff and school leaders, there would be no other professions. No civilised society, for that matter.

'Retirement Tales' has been a celebration of education - a love story, if you will. It's been a celebration of life too. Life is fleeting and fragile; we don't get that long to make a difference so we should make all our words and actions count.

To all our followers: thank you! Your company has been a greater blessing than you will ever know.

To all those working in childcare and education: thank you! Please keep doing what you do. Children need you. The world needs you.

We wish you all the best. Geoff and Margaret.

#whatwouldgeoffdo
#bemoreMargaret

Chapter 6: Adventures in Advent

Over the years, Margaret has incurred the wrath of caretakers for using too much glitter and the wrath of headteachers for spending too many weeks on the Nativity.

But the autumn second half term has always been one of her favourites.

She is really looking forward to The Call.

💬   🔁   ♡   ⬆️

Margaret affectionately refers to the period between November 6th and November 30th as Advent Advent.

"I'm counting down to counting down to Christmas, Geoff!"

If you wish to join in with Advent, you can open the first door of your first calendar today!

💬   🔁   ♡   ⬆️

History was on the timetable today. Margaret was thrilled! The theme was "Toys". There were no videos of Magic Grandad so Margaret took the class back in time herself.
The children talked about Lego and Margaret enthused about a construction toy called Bayko.
She's magic, Margaret.

💬   🔁   ♡   ⬆️

One box.
Six rubber stamps.

Lots of school Christmas
memories!

Margaret says, if you're having
a toy day at the end of term,
remind your children of some
basic rules:

1. Nothing with batteries
   (eg Speak & Spell).
2. Nothing noisy
   (especially Hungry Hippos).
3. Nothing with too many parts
   (ie Mousetrap).
4. Etch-a-Sketch is a safe bet.

Good news for game lovers!
The Education Secretary edition of "Guess Who?" is available
now!

Featuring ten of the most recent post holders, some of whom
you might even recognise.

You know the Christmas Story very well but it's probably quite a few years since you've seen a Banda printed, purple ink version!

Margaret says she can virtually smell the Banda fluid...
...and the wax crayons.

Chapter Seven:
The Old School Christmas Assembly

It was on a starry night...

Margaret and I are delighted to confirm that we will be hosting an Old School Christmas Assembly, live on Twitter, on Thursday 8th December, at 8pm.

We've got two weeks to find an overhead projector and a glockenspiel...

Thursday 8th December, at 8pm

Geoff and Margaret's
Old School Christmas Assembly

There are just nine days until we host our Old School Christmas Assembly!

Today, the Lovely Head is loaning us his school hall and old piano. Margaret is armed with four classic music books.

It's rehearsal time!

Margaret and I have spent much of the day rehearsing songs and working out the logistics for our Old School Christmas Assembly.

I can confirm that the piano is out of tune, the overhead projector is temperamental and there isn't one complete glockenspiel to be found anywhere.

○ ⟲ ♡ ⬆

It's rehearsal day!

Margaret and I will be spending the day holed up in a secret location (the Lovely Head's school hall). We'll be running through all the songs and logistics for tomorrow night's Old School Christmas Assembly.

There will be chime bars, guitars and faux pas.

○ ⟲ ♡ ⬆

Geoff & Margaret's
♫ Old School Christmas Assembly ♫

🎄 Thursday 8th December at 8.00pm 🎄

Music: Merry Christmas Everyone - Shakin' Stevens

Welcome - Geoff

Song - Gabriel's Message

Notice - P.T.A.

Reading: The First Christmas (Pt 1) - Special Guest

Song - Little Donkey

Reading: The First Christmas (Pt 2)

Song - It Was On A Starry Night

Song - Calypso Carol (See Him Lying...)

Reading: The First Christmas (Pt 3)

Song - The Virgin Mary Had a Baby Boy
(with Percussion Club)

A Christmas Prayer - Special Guest

Final Song - Away in a Manger

The Old School Christmas Assembly

Introduction

It's time to bring some Joy to the World! It's time for
Geoff and Margaret's Old School Assembly!
Welcome one and all!

Here's a festive pop classic to listen to while you take your seats (or floorspace):

Margaret loves that song and she loves Shakin' Stevens!

"Not many people can pull off the double denim look, Geoff...only Shakey...

...and Headteacher Halil..."

Welcome

It's great to have so many of you with us for this festive evening but it is a bit of a squash here in the hall. Feel free to sit on the wooden benches at the back if you need a bit more leg room!

Please remember, if you do end up on the benches, it doesn't mean this is a PE lesson. We don't expect anyone to just be in vest and pants today. Some people should be in dressing gowns though.

If you are sitting on the hall floor, our Site Manager has asked me to remind you not to pick at the parquet. It's in need of a polish.

Song

Our first song tonight is "Gabriel's Message", from the festive music book Merrily to Bethlehem. Please could our Overhead Projector Monitors get ready for their duties?

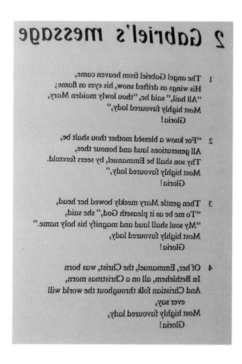

Please accept our apologies for the issues with the overhead projector during that first song. The monitors are a little out of practice.

You all did really well at singing along to the back-to-front acetate.

It's just like old times!

Notice

Before we continue, members of the PTA have asked me to remind you that they have a stall selling mince pies, sherry and sugar mice at the end of the assembly.

All money raised will go towards the school buying a new big TV and video recorder.

Now, in this assembly, we'll be singing some of your favourite school Christmas songs and creating a Nativity tableau.

There will be tea towels, chime bars and the odd faux pas. But remember, it's not a pantomime...

Bible Reading

We're now going to hear the first part of the story of the First Christmas, from the Good News Bible:

Thank you, Mr Theobalds, for reading for us all this evening. What a fine Lancashire accent you have!

Song

Our next carol is Little Donkey.
Please leave space down the middle of the hall for Mary, Joseph and their little donkey to pass. Over to the Projector Monitors...
--
Apologies to those children next to the aisle who the donkey trod on. This is why we always say to cross your legs in assembly.

Bible Reading

It's time for another Bible reading now!

Please could our junior readers come to the front? The reading is taken from Luke, Chapter2...

--

Well done to our Year 6 readers! Didn't they read clearly?

Don't worry, we won't be asking any questions about fronted adverbials.

Song

It's time to sing again! Margaret has asked me to remind everyone to sit up straight while you sing!

Our shepherds will be making their way down the sides of the hall during this next song.

It was on a Starry Night...

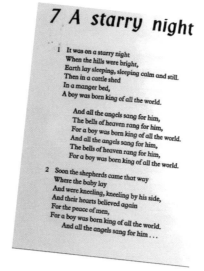

7 A starry night

1 It was on a starry night
   When the hills were bright,
   Earth lay sleeping, sleeping calm and still.
   Then in a cattle shed
   In a manger bed,
   A boy was born king of all the world.

   And all the angels sang for him,
   The bells of heaven rang for him,
   For a boy was born king of all the world.
   And all the angels sang for him,
   The bells of heaven rang for him,
   For a boy was born king of all the world.

2 Soon the shepherds came that way
   Where the baby lay
   And were kneeling, kneeling by his side,
   And their hearts believed again
   For the peace of men,
   For a boy was born king of all the world.
   And all the angels sang for him . . .

I forgot to introduce our rhythm section before that song. Well done to everyone playing along with castanets, rhythm sticks and fidget toys.

Song

Our next song is Calypso Carol.
Margaret says you might know this as "See Him Lying on a Bed of Straw".
--
Well done, everyone! You all sounded great!
And that brass band was a wonderful surprise!
We should give a special mention to our Projector Monitors who got the words the right way round.

Bible Reading

We're now going to have the third part of the story of the First Christmas. We had invited Nursery Nurse Doris to read this passage but her IBS has flared up and she doesn't really want to stand at the front. Instead, we'll put the words on the projector & we'll all read together.

The reading is taken from the Gospel of Matthew: Chapter 2 v 1-12

--

Goodness, that was a long reading! We're even closer to Christmas now.

Song

It's time to sing again and this time we are going to be joined by our Percussion Club. Margaret says please be kind if things don't sound perfect. We've only had one rehearsal of this song and it was via Zoom.

Carol: The Virgin Mary Had a Baby Boy

Here we go!

...

What a performance!
Well done to our Wise Men for improvising during that song!
They were supposed to come from the East.
I'm sorry the fire door was blocked and you had to walk all the way round from the West.

Prayer

It's time to pray now.
Margaret and I would like to thank the Revd Mary Hawes for offering this prayer, especially for our assembly.
Hands together and eyes closed!

Dear God,
Thank you for Christmas. Thank you for the excitement of parties and presents and decorations. Thank you that they help us to celebrate Jesus' birthday.
You sent Jesus to show how much you love us. Help us to show that love to people who will struggle this Christmas, including those who won't have lots of presents or party food.
Amen

Final Song

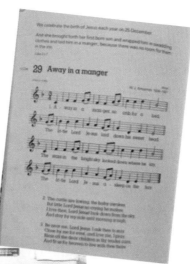

Our final song tonight is the much-loved carol, Away in a Manger.
Please join in with the words on the screen, for one last time.

What a special arrangement that was!
--
Thank you, everyone, for taking part in our assembly this evening. We hope you've enjoyed it!

22 Dec 22

Here's a Christmas card from me
and Margaret!

We wish you joy and peace this
Christmas time.

(There's a £1 note inside the card.
Treat yourself to something nice.)

HAPPY CHRISTMAS
from Geoff & Margaret

---

31 Dec 22

And just like that a year has passed!
Margaret & I have had a year of answering
"The Call".
We've had a year of Tweeting our tales and reflections.
We've seen off two Prime Ministers,
four Education Secretaries and one attempt
at being banned from Twitter.

It's always been about joy & hope.

*The end of term
and the end of part three*

Epilogue: Where It All Began

GOV.UK

| Department for Education

This is your daily email to keep you updated on the government's response to coronavirus (COVID-19)

Dear School Leaders,

The Department understands that you will have been waiting for official advice, in relation to returning for the start of the new term. We have been considering the very latest Government data before issuing our guidance to schools.

We can now confirm that 3 people in every 2 currently have a positive Covid result. This is mathematically unusual but a discussion around these numbers will form a fun part of any maths mastery work.

The fact that there are now more cases than people could potentially impact on the provision of education in a minority of settings. With no children present and no staff to teach, schools should put in place measures to keep schools operating fully. This might involve employing animals to teach and using EYFS dolls and puppets as pupils. Phonics teaching should continue as normal and an additional screening test will take place later in the year.

It is vital that all accountability measures remain in place throughout these uncertain times. With that in mind, we will be reducing the Ofsted inspection cycle and increasing the length of inspections. There will be deep dives where you least expect them, including the canteen, the staff room and that cupboard in the ICT suite.

The regular Ofsted workforce has been significantly affected by Covid related absence. So that schools don't miss out, the inspectorate has been supplemented by a pool of retired inspectors, demoted Education Secretaries and local freemasons. Ask no questions.

We did previously articulate that school employees were no more at risk from Covid than adults in any other workplaces. This was, in hindsight, a slight miscalculation. This is why we have led a huge national drive to recruit an army of ex-teachers back in to the profession. The Department can confirm that the marketing campaign has been an unprecedented success. Geoff and Margaret have both said "yes" and are available for work at schools up and down the ~~country~~ ~~county~~ town street.

We wish you a happy new year.

ps SATs week will be in May, as usual.

Dedications

This book is dedicated to educators everywhere,
to everyone who wants to change the world
and to anybody whose life was changed by Covid-19.